Praise for *Race, Sports, a...*

"Sports and education should represent a powerful and positive alliance. Singer demonstrates how wrong it can all go when ideas about race and property intersect. This is a must-read for educators, athletics professionals, and parents who are encouraging their children to pursue sports careers."

—**Gloria Ladson-Billings**, *professor emerita,*
University of Wisconsin–Madison

"Unsparing in its critique of the significance of race in the 'collegiate sports industrial complex' but abidingly optimistic in its final outlook, *Race, Sports, and Education* brings the debate over the status and circumstances of Black male collegiate athletes into the twenty-first century."

—**Harry Edwards**, *professor emeritus, sociology, University of California,*
Berkeley, and consultant for the NFL, NBA, NCAA College/University

"*Race, Sports, and Education* gives a voice to the voiceless through the words of Black male athletes."

—**John Shoop**, *former NFL and college football coach*

"John Singer puts forward an essential truth: that to find pathways to advance justice and equality for African American male college athletes, the issue of race must be placed at the center. He weaves a compelling story that confronts the forces of white supremacy and racialized hierarchies that create an exploitative college sport system and exact inestimable harms on the human dignity, possibility, and worth of not just African American players but all those who have an investment in coming to terms with the legacy of race in America."

—**Ellen J. Staurowsky**, *professor, Department of Sport*
Management, Lebow College of Business, Drexel University

"Singer's brilliance is evidenced in prose, in expert analysis, and in his skillful presentation of compelling counternarratives. This important volume complicates what we know about how race, sports, and education commingle."

—**Shaun R. Harper**, *founder and executive director, University of Southern California Race and Equity Center*

"The academic talent development of Black male college athletes remains grossly understudied and poorly documented. John Singer's new text is a timely and welcome entry for that critical knowledge gap."

—**Eddie Comeaux**, *editor of College Athletes' Rights and Well-Being*

Race, Sports,
and Education

SERIES | RACE AND EDUCATION

Series edited by H. Richard Milner IV

OTHER BOOKS IN THIS SERIES

Race, Sports, and Education

Improving Opportunities and Outcomes for Black Male College Athletes

John N. Singer

Harvard Education Press
Cambridge, Massachusetts

Paperback ISBN 978-1-68253-409-0
Library Edition ISBN 978-1-68253-410-6

Library of Congress Cataloging-in-Publication Data is on file.

Names: Singer, John N. (John Nathaniel), 1973- author.
Title: Race, sports, and education : improving opportunities and outcomes for black male college athletes / John N. Singer.
Description: Cambridge, Massachusetts : Harvard Education Press, [2019] | Series: Race and education series | Includes bibliographical references and index. | Summary: "Race, Sports, and Education highlights the myriad ways in which organized collegiate sport has both positively contributed to and negatively detracted from the educational experiences of Black male college athletes. Specifically, John N. Singer examines the educational experiences, opportunities, and outcomes of Black males who have played NCAA Division I football and/or basketball at historically White colleges and universities. Singer is intensely aware of the ways in which many Black athletes have been shortchanged by the collegiate sport system. He describes how the colleges and universities have exploited athletes for the institutions' financial gain and deprived them of basic educational opportunities that ought to be enjoyed by all students. At the same time, Singer argues that sports do in fact offer genuine educational opportunities and benefits for many of these athletes. He is acutely attuned to the fact that these athletes love their sports, and that their participation in these sports makes unique educational experiences available to them. As Singer shows, to understand the situation and to chart realistic, fruitful reform measures requires a full appreciation of the complexity-indeed, of the many competing and contradictory elements-that characterizes intercollegiate sport and the experiences of Black athletes at the present time. The book brings to the fore the voices, stories, and perspectives of twelve Black male college athletes via a case study of teammates from a big-time college football program and individual reflective vignettes of athletes across several different college programs. Through his analysis of the system and his attention to student views and experiences, Singer crafts a valuable, nuanced account and points in the direction of reforms that would significantly improve the educational opportunities and experiences of these athletes. At a time when collegiate sports have attained unmistakable institutional value and generated unprecedented financial returns-all while largely failing the educational needs of its athletes-this book offers a clear, detailed vision of the current situation and suggestions for a more equitable way forward"— Provided by publisher.
Identifiers: LCCN 2019025117 | ISBN 9781682534090 (paperback) | ISBN 9781682534106 (library binding)
Subjects: LCSH: African American male college students. | African American male college students—Case studies. | African American college athletes. | African American college athletes—Case studies. | School improvement programs—United States. | School improvement programs—United States—Case studies. | Racism in sports—United States. | Racism in sports—United States—Case studies.
Classification: LCC LC2781 .S553 2019 | DDC 378.1982996073—dc23
LC record available at https://lccn.loc.gov/2019025117

Published by Harvard Education Press,
an imprint of the Harvard Education Publishing Group

Harvard Education Press
8 Story Street
Cambridge, MA 02138

Cover Design: Ciano Design
Cover Photo: RichVintage/E+/Getty Images
The typefaces used in this book are Minion Pro and Myriad Pro

This book is dedicated to Black male college athletes—past, present, and future—whose collective athletic prowess, intellect, and mighty presence on campuses and in athletic departments across historically White US institutions of higher education has literally and figuratively changed the face and trajectory of college sport over the past several decades.

Contents

Series Foreword

by H. Richard Milner IV
Race and Education Series Editor

A FEW DAYS AGO, I walked into a barbershop that serves mostly Black patrons for my biweekly haircut. In some public contexts, when I walk into a room as an "education professor" or "teacher," I tend to be inundated with questions about education. These questions range from what is happening in the local Nashville Public Schools to national topics such as the recent college admissions cheating scandal. Indeed, people expect me to have an opinion, insight, and even direction for just about anything regarding education. However, in the barbershop, I become part of a powerful fabric of other Black bodies, usually talking about sport. That my most recent visit to the barbershop happened to occur during March Madness meant that there was an intense focus on the top college basketball teams making their journeys from the sweet 16, to the elite 8, then final 4, and eventually the championship.

As a qualitative researcher, I am struck by and drawn especially to these conversations among those in the barbershop (with most of whom I do not have a relationship). I observe and listen intently to their conjectures about the upcoming games. I listen to their analyses of previous games, which address coaches' decisions or players' three-point averages. I pay attention to their word choices as they consider their top picks for the National Basketball Association (NBA) draft—on this day, Duke University's Zion Williamson was "sure to be the top pick in the draft." But what is also nothing short of fascinating as I observe and "study" the discursive interactions between and among those Black bodies are the seamless ways in which they talk sport *and race*, which in their talk meet—and intersect—within a space of confluence: they run as flowingly as a steep stream.

Although they don't name it as such, these Black bodies in the barbershop draw from theory—often tenets of critical race theory—as they discuss the intersections of race and sport. They draw from established and powerful evidence spaces. They draw from statistics from previous games. They build on stories—nuanced narratives they have heard or read about. They build on patterns they have observed themselves in players over time. And they make sense of their predictions based on their own experiences as those who have played sport, coached their children in Little League games, and/or observed different sports for many years. And these people substantiate their discussions about sport and race based on their *raced* experiences. They draw from the fact that they have been marginalized and still experience racism. They make connections between how White privilege emerges in their places of work, outside of sport. They speculate about how racism is permanent and omnipresent in society, as critical race theorist Derrick Bell has stressed.[1]

Take a stroll into many, if not most, Black barbershops across the US—during basketball or football seasons, especially—and there will typically be spirited discussions about sport. And there will be real conversations about *race and sport*. The discussions I hear, from "elders" and "youngsters" alike, focus on the broad and the specific. The discourse is filled with the mundane and the serious. It is refreshing to observe that, unlike others, these Black people do not shy away from the ways in which race and racism manifest in the experiences of players (and their families), coaches, managers, and owners. It is also reassuring to hear how these Black people talk about how rules, policies, and mechanisms are also raced, who has a seat at the table to decide whether a Colin Kaepernick or others will be allowed to use their bodies to fight against injustice in society. There are multiple layers of expertise in Black barbershops—insights from which any of us might learn. Indeed, language and literacy scholar Yolanda Majors, in her book *Shoptalk: Lessons in Teaching from an African American Hair Salon*, shares the richness of community and collective African American knowledge that emerges in spaces of agency, expertise, and shared culture, such as beauty salons.[2]

However, some would argue that sport, similar to problematic discourses related to the field of mathematics, is neutral. Some would suggest that sport, like problematic discourses related to education, is the great equalizer. But John N. Singer brilliantly argues in *Race, Sports, and*

Education that to deeply understand history and current movements inside and outside of sport, race has to be interrogated. With no apology, Singer advances a powerful narrative that race should, in fact, be front and center when considering agendas to advance equity and justice.

Drawing from the voices of Black male athletes over time, he studies the ways in which these athletes complicate and nuance the "student" in student-athlete. In what ways, for instance, are Black students implicitly encouraged to prioritize sports over their academic expectations? How does the institution of college sport exploit particular bodies—especially Black bodies—to maintain a form of university and higher educational capitalism that benefits the White majority? How can we not consider our moral compasses when we allow Black athletes—through big-time college sports such as basketball and football—to live in poverty, sometimes struggling to make ends meet while the university benefits from their labor? How do we reconcile the reality that too many Black athletes will never graduate and most will not reach the pinnacle of sport to earn a living after graduation? What Singer has done in this book is to privilege the voices and perspectives of those who matter most—the athletes themselves—as they work through racist systems inside of *sport* as well as in *academics*. Written with passion and purpose, this book reminds us of the myriad ways in which Black athletes navigate and negotiate three permeable cites of racism: society, athletics, and academics.

But rather than simply pointing out the many issues, phobias, spaces of discrimination, and challenges we face regarding race and racism in sport, athletics, and higher education, Singer provides recommendations and implications for disrupting systems, policies, and practices that maintain the status quo. The book is a remarkable exemplar of Freire's wisdom: the answers and solutions to challenges in a community are found in the very spaces of the challenges.[3] This book is a must-read for educators and students at the secondary and postsecondary level. College athletes (past, present, and future), coaches, athletics administrators, counselors, boosters, academic support personnel for athletes, and parents and families supporting athletic programs should read this book. Indeed, it represents a refreshing call to know and more deeply understand a complicated truth about the salience of race and sport. *Race, Sports, and Education* enters the Race and Education Series at a time when we need to reimage sport in the spirit of justice for all.

Introduction

This college sports system contributes to the undervaluing of black lives in American society and our institutions. The predominantly white privilege of playing college sports while earning a quality degree comes at the expense of—is literally *paid for by*—the educationally unequal experiences of mostly black football and basketball players.

Victoria L. Jackson[1]

It's five types of ball players: Volley, foot, soccer, basket, base all in the same race to win. What happens when the clock stops, injury, and no more wicked jump shots?

ESPN ends; there goes your two million fans and there goes your friends.

They don't care who you are and what you did. You a "Where are they now?" VH-1 type kid.

Erick Sermon[2]

What happens to the subjugated racial minority in the nominally integrated and systematically exploitive system does not just happen to them; it just happens to them first and worst. Ultimately, it negatively influences the fate and fortunes of all who share a comparable position with that minority.

Harry Edwards[3]

S INCE THE LATE 1960s INTO THE 1970s, when Black males were beginning to routinely integrate as athletes into football and basketball programs at historically White colleges and universities (HWCU) that sponsor National Collegiate Athletic Association (NCAA) Division I sport programs in the US, the educational plight of the Black male athletes in these programs has been a popular topic of inquiry and discussion.[4] Sociologist and scholar activist Harry Edwards's pioneering work at the intersection of race, sport, and US society has helped set the tone for the formal study and heightened interest in Black male athletes' educational experiences and outcomes at HWCU.[5] Many scholars, journalists, and other social commentators now regularly debate these matters at academic and industry conferences, in college and university classrooms, on television and other media, and in scholarly journals and the popular press, among other places.

Since 2000, there have also been noteworthy books that devote substantial attention to Black male football and basketball athletes in US higher education. In his 2007 book, *Race, Sport, and the American Dream*, sociologist Earl Smith focused on Black males' position within what he termed the *athletics industrial complex*, which "refers to the fact that intercollegiate athletics is now firmly embedded into other economic institutions from the hotel and entertainment industry to construction to clothing and transportation."[6] Smith argues that the athletics industrial complex is the primary mechanism that drives the exploitation and colonization of Black male bodies, planting them firmly in the "periphery" of the college sport economy. Billy Hawkins's 2010 book, *The New Plantation*, builds on this notion of colonization in big-time college sport by providing critical insight into how structural arrangements at HWCU present extraordinary challenges to Black male football and basketball athletes' educational opportunities. Hawkins emphasizes the need for decolonization and concludes with strong recommendations for college athletic reform.[7] In *Black Males and Intercollegiate Athletics*, a multiauthored book published in 2015, contributors explore effective ways to address issues facing Black male athletes, focusing on the critical roles coaches, faculty, administrators, academic support staff, and athletes themselves play in this collective process of serving the educational interests and needs of this important student population. The foreword by Maurice Clarett (a former football running back who helped lead the Ohio State Buckeyes to the national championship during his freshman year in 2002), presents a powerful and authentic voice for introducing readers to the themes and topics in the book.[8] In particular, Clarett speaks about the critical need for Black male athletes to develop a support network of people outside athletics, and encourages these athletes and their support network to use the book to educate themselves and engage in conversations about ways to address problems facing Black male athletes in these spaces. Lastly, Joseph Cooper's book *From Exploitation*

Back to Empowerment draws from an array of analytic frameworks to discuss the heterogeneity of Black male athletes' experiences and outcomes over the course of their lives and proposes multiple socialization models to help explain holistic development processes for Black male athletes.[9]

Despite the abundant attention that has thus far been paid to the educational plight of Black male college athletes, and the excellent research on the topic, there remains a great deal more to be said. I hope what I have to share will add value and substance to what has already been written or said about Black male college athletes. Our knowledge of matters related to their education is incomplete, and is certainly not absolute. The voices of countless Black male college athletes have gone unheard, and this gap must be filled; there is always more to know and learn about this topic. In this regard, the ongoing study of Black male athletes' education undoubtedly still matters.

Furthermore, in this era of Black Lives Matter, where White supremacists' violence and the discriminatory legislation directed toward Black people not only persist but are intensifying, Black male athletes' education requires our increased attention. The exploitation of Black male football and basketball athlete labor continues to be at the center of the increasing hyper-commercialism we have witnessed in this academic capitalist governance model of college sport.

The NCAA and its member institutions continue to peddle rhetoric about the importance of providing college athletes with well-rounded educational experiences and opportunities to help prepare them "to go pro in something other than sports," as the television commercial goes. Unfortunately, there continue to be far too many instances where Black male football and basketball athletes at HWCU are treated by leaders and other professional practitioners in these institutions as if their education does not matter and is not important to their short- and long-term life opportunities and outcomes beyond college sport participation. In a provocative article on Black Lives Matter, T. Elon Dancy and colleagues draw from theories of settler colonialism and anti-Blackness to (re)interpret the arrangements between HWCU and Black people. These scholars strongly suggest that the academy's commitment to White entitlement, Black male bodies as commodities, and rejection of Black intellect is arguably most pervasive in college football and men's basketball at HWCU, which is one reason I focus on these two sports in this book.[10] In the quote at the outset of this chapter, Victoria Jackson, a former Division I college track and field athlete turned sports historian, echoes this sentiment. In chapter 4, I will revisit this point and other related arguments.

WHO IS THIS BOOK FOR?

This book will be highly relevant and relatable to other scholars and academics who study and teach in areas such as higher education; urban education; sociology of education; sport studies including management, sociology, psychology, philosophy, history; and Black or Africana or other racial and ethnic studies. However, *Race, Sports, and Education* is particularly aimed at educational decision makers and other stakeholders who work or interact directly with Black male athletes in higher education—athletics administrators, coaches, academic support, and other higher education practitioners—as well as administrators, teachers, coaches, academic guidance counselors and other educational stakeholders at the secondary level of P–12 schooling who are responsible for helping to prepare Black male athletes for their transition into institutions of higher education. It is also written specifically for former, current, and future Black male college athletes and their support networks, particularly family and friends. Athletes from other racial and gender backgrounds might find the content of this book useful as well.

Much of the material presented in this book is generated directly from the stories and words of the Black male college athletes who are featured in chapters 2 and 3. Accordingly, I draw heavily on the perspectives of these athletes to provide critical insight from which athletics administrators, coaches, academic support for athletics personnel, and other higher education practitioners might learn. Reading and engaging with the content of this book might help these important leaders and professional practitioners address the inequitable or unjust systems that have served as barriers that prevent Black male athletes and some of their athlete peers from maximizing their educational opportunities.

Therefore, the primary focus of this book is on what higher education practitioners and their counterparts in P–12 education might learn from the voices and perspectives of this historically underserved student group. I hope that these leaders and practitioners will also find useful strategies or recommendations for what they can do to advance the educational experiences and outcomes for Black male athletes and their peers. Herein lies one of the major contributions this book will make to the scholarly literature and everyday conversations about Black male athlete education matters.

SITUATING MYSELF IN THE DISCOURSE

Throughout *Race, Sports, and Education*, I acknowledge and discuss synergies and overlap between this book and the work of the scholars mentioned above. I also explore how this book builds on and in some ways departs from the prior work related to the education of Black male college athletes.

This book draws from precepts of *critical race theory* (CRT) and other related works to examine pertinent macro-, meso-, and micro-level matters that impact educational experiences and outcomes of Black male college athletes. CRT scholars draw from centuries of evidence to understand how a system of White supremacy and racial hierarchies have been established and implanted in US society, especially via the legal system; and they work to disrupt this systemic racism and other forms of oppression that subordinate and marginalize certain groups and individuals. In line with CRT, I embrace an anti-deficit approach instead of focusing on the supposed deficiencies or shortcomings of Black male college athletes, who education scholar Shaun Harper suggested are the most disenfranchised student group in higher education.[11] An anti-deficit approach focuses more on their strengths, untapped assets and attributes, and potential for greatness in higher education and life beyond. This approach is one that education scholar Fred Bonner promoted in *Building on Resilience*, which offers models by different authors that might contribute to Black male success in P–12 and higher education contexts.[12]

My embrace of this approach does not mean, however, that I fail to acknowledge or discuss what decades of literature says about Black male football and basketball athletes as a group ranking at the very bottom of most socially constructed academic indicators of success such as GPA, standardized test scores, or graduation rates. I am also well aware that some Black male athletes do come to HWCU with limited academic preparation and/or very little interest in anything beyond playing football or basketball. In acknowledging this, however, my attention and critique is directed more toward significant historical and contemporary issues at the societal and sport industry levels (macro-level matters) and the cultures, climates, structures, policies, processes, and practices within college sport organizations, particularly the NCAA and HWCU athletic departments (meso-level matters) that impact the education of Black male athletes. Essentially, this book places more emphasis on what is "wrong" with the broader US society and educational and sport enterprises, as opposed to what is "wrong" with Black male athletes, who since their full-scale integration into HWCU have played the leading role in helping grow college sport into the multibillion-dollar entity it has become. I draw inspiration from and build on Harry Edwards's argument that (so-called) Black male "dumb jocks" are not born, but are systematically created.[13]

PURPOSE AND SCOPE OF BOOK

The purpose of *Race, Sports, and Education* is twofold. First, I critically examine educational experiences and outcomes of Black males who played NCAA Division I football and/or basketball at HWCU.[14] Although I incorporate my own personal and professional experiences and theoretically informed perspectives, I center the discourse on the voices and perspectives of the twelve Black male college athletes via a case study (chapter 2) and individual reflective narrative vignettes (chapter 3).[15] In particular, I share their stories about P–12 schooling and sport experiences, pertinent education matters and challenges they faced as college athletes, their perspectives on how college sport impacted their education and life after college sport, and recommendations they have for reform aimed at addressing Black male athlete education matters. In many ways, this book responds to the rhetorical questions hip-hop rap artist Erick Sermon posed in the quote at the beginning of this chapter. That is, these Black males provide insight into the question, "What happens when the clock stops?" after their playing days have officially ended. My co-creation of knowledge about education matters with these Black males is one of the major strengths and contributions of the book. I believe this is one of the things that helps distinguish it from other books related to this topic.

Second, I explore more satisfactory and equitable ways HWCU and their athletic departments can serve the educational interests and needs of

Black male athletes who come through these programs. The book addresses the persistent educational disparities between Black male football and basketball athletes and their college athlete peers from other racial and gender backgrounds and in athletic programs beyond football and men's basketball. In doing so, I argue Harry Edwards's assertion that Black male football and basketball athletes at HWCU are typically the "first" targets of exploitation, and their educational experiences and outcomes as a group continue to be the "worst" in comparison to their peers is still relevant today and remains a pressing matter.

I want to be clear, though, that this is not a doom-and-gloom book that views college sport as being totally devoid of redeeming qualities and attributes, or Black male college athletes as helpless victims who are incapable of traversing the world of college sport at HWCU. On the contrary, this book reveals how Black male athletes have grappled with the ugly sides of college sport that too often negatively affect their educational experiences and outcomes as a group. The athletes featured in this book have parlayed their college sport participation into meaningful educational experiences and life lessons going forward. By highlighting their stories of educational excellence and resilience, even in the face of structural barriers and constraints within these systems, the book helps illuminate how and why some Black male college athletes have had success navigating the myriad challenges and opportunities they were presented with during their playing days and in life transitions afterward.

While the focal point of this book is college sport, it does touch on how educational pipeline matters (e.g., P–12 schooling, socialization forces, and experiences outside of schools) serve as precursors to these challenges and opportunities. The discussion allows for a critical investigation into some of the complex and contextual realities of Black male college athletes' relationships with college sport in particular, and the US educational and sport systems more broadly.

Race, Sports, and Education argues there is a need for systems and learning environments to be constructed and sustained by leaders and professional practitioners in higher (and secondary) education that help nurture and extract from Black male athletes the unique gifts and talents beyond the athletic prowess they possess. There is most certainly educational value in sport participation and competition on the fields and courts of play. However I agree with Joseph Cooper's strong call that there is a need to focus on "excellence beyond athletics" if we are truly interested in the education of Black male college athletes and their peers.[16]

Moreover, while the traditional classroom setting is a staple of students' educational experiences and outcomes, true education goes beyond just the teaching and learning of the subjects in the school curriculum that will help students graduate and enter a career; it also involves students' exposure to environments and situations where they can discover their history, who they are, and what their purpose in life is and gain knowledge of the world around them. Education involves the cultivation of students' inner gifts and talents via their exposure to various bodies of knowledge, fields of human endeavor, and diverse people, places, things, ideas, and experiences. In this regard, education of Black male athletes should occur not only on the field or court and in the university classroom, but also in myriad other social contexts within and outside institutions of higher education.

With all that in mind, this book also acknowledges and discusses the ultimate responsibility Black male college athletes have to pursue and contribute to their own education. Harry Edwards articulated this point decades ago when he stated:

> It is the black student-athletes themselves who must shoulder a substantial portion of the responsibility for improving their own circumstances. Education is an activist pursuit and cannot in reality be "given." It must be obtained "the old-fashion way"—one must earn it . . . the bottom line here is that if black student-athletes fail to take an active role in establishing and legitimizing a priority upon academic achievement, nothing done by any other party to this American sports tragedy will matter—if for no other reason than the fact that a slave cannot be freed against his will.[17]

I do not believe Edwards was in any way absolving educational institutions of their responsibility to create the proper conditions and circumstances for Black male athletes to obtain academic achievement and other educational outcomes. Rather, he seems to suggest that Black athletes must expect more from and rely more on themselves than these HWCU do if they truly desire the kind of education that is necessary for them to lead productive and wholesome lives beyond sport participation.

WHAT ABOUT BLACK FEMALES AND OTHER COLLEGE ATHLETES?

In March 2016, I drove Harry Edwards back to the airport after he gave a lecture at Texas A&M University. In that talk, he compared and contrasted Black athlete activism on college campuses during the Black Power movement in the civil rights era with that of the more recent Black Lives Matter movement in the age of social media.[18] On our two-hour ride back to Austin, I decided to share my idea for this book and get his initial thoughts about it. He suggested that I not limit this project to just Black males, but instead consider writing about the intersections between race, sport, and education in regard to the experiences and outcomes of male and female athletes across various demographic backgrounds and types of sports.

To me, Dr. Edwards is an intellectual giant whom I greatly respect and look up to both literally and figuratively, and whose work I first encountered and studied as an undergraduate and graduate student in the 1990s and early 2000s. He makes a vital point that we should pay more attention to the roles and experiences of Black females in sport, education, and society. In some of his more recent work, Edwards has called for a paradigm shift to focus more on women and girls. He discussed his observations from the Black Student-Athlete Conference: Challenges and Opportunities at the University of Texas at Austin in 2015, and expressed some frustration with the overwhelming attention on Black males and limited attention given to Black females.[19]

Many other sport scholars have pointed out how Black females are a population of college athletes who have not received the kind of attention in either the popular press or the academic literature that they deserve. In 2005, sport management scholar Jennifer Bruening (now McGarry) posed the question, "Are all the women Whites and all the Blacks men?" in furthering the call for Black females to be more central and visible in sport studies.[20] Other scholars have critically examined important matters related to Black females in college sport. Akilah Carter-Francique's important scholarship and service work with Black female college athletes particularly comes to mind. She has built on earlier foundational work of scholars such as Yevonne Smith, Doris Corbett, and Tina Sloan Green, and has been committed for several years to the study with and empowerment of this important college student population.[21]

I further recognize that other athletes across various social groups and identity spectrums are susceptible to the exploitive nature of the college sport system, and there is a need to include these different athlete groups in our work on education matters in college sport. As an example, important work on educational challenges specific to Asian/Pacific Islander college football athletes has emerged in the academic literature.[22] The success of former Heisman Trophy–winning college quarterback Marcus Mariota at the University of Oregon from 2012 to 2014 and the rapid emergence and subsequent dominance of University of Alabama quarterback Tua Tagovailoa beginning in early 2018 has certainly helped bring more attention to and interest in this particular population of college athletes.

Yet in the end, I chose in this book not to follow Edwards's advice. I am unapologetic about and remain steadfast in my commitment to centering Black male college athletes' education matters. I also argue that doing so could actually help achieve meaningful reform for the benefit of all college athletes. As a Black male, my deep and ongoing interest in the study of and with Black male athletes does not mean that I do not understand or appreciate the plight of my beloved Black female counterparts. From my perspective, Black males and females are in a collective struggle and real fight against the forces of what the late great rapper Tupac Shakur called this "White man'z world" and sociologists Joe Feagin and Kimberly Ducey framed as the elite White male dominance system.[23] As I will discuss in more detail throughout this book, this sophisticated and extensive system of oppression and subjugation was not designed by or for Black males and females, nor to serve the interests of either group. Whether we focus our attention and analysis on Black male or female athletes separately or simultaneously, there is a need for the continued and vigorous study of education and other matters pertaining to Black people in this system—period! In this regard, I do not view my focus in this book on Black male college athletes as a slight against or erasure of their female or other counterparts.

THE ELITE WHITE MALE DOMINANCE SYSTEM AND COLLEGE SPORT

To discuss the circumstances of Black male athletes at HWCU, it is first necessary to trace and interrogate the elite White male dominance system that has long permeated US society and social institutions, including college sport.[24] In their book *Elite White Men Ruling*, Joe Feagin and Kimberley Ducey argue that public and scholarly discussions of US racism and other forms of oppression have, for the most part, failed to foreground elite White men and focus on how their interlocking racial, class, and gender statuses impact their global power and influence: "The central problem of the 21st century is elite white men. They long ago created what we term the *elite-white-male dominance system*, a complex and oppressive system central to most western societies that now affects much of the planet. This small elite rules actively, undemocratically, and globally, yet remains largely invisible to the billions of people it routinely dominates."

Feagin and Ducey described elite White males as those individuals who are at the very top of the social and economic order of societies and of social institutions. Higher education and college sport certainly qualify as powerful social institutions, particularly in the US. White males have always held and continue to hold the overwhelming majority of the major leadership and decision-making positions in the upper echelons of higher education and college sport. Although some remain relatively out of the public eye, in some cases they are highly visible public figures in roles such as college and university chancellors or presidents, the NCAA president, athletic conference commissioners, athletic directors, and head football and basketball coaches. It may be difficult to tell whether or not these public figures are elites themselves or influential acolytes of elite White males who remain invisible and behind the scenes. In college sport, such acolytes typically comprise people from various racial and gender backgrounds who are not necessarily at the top of the social and economic order, but are in managerial and other important roles within athletic departments and other organizations tied to the college sport industry segment. They perpetuate the system by carrying out the agenda of the elite White men at the top of these organizations by implementing certain rules, regulations, policies, processes, and day-to-day practices that ultimately and primarily serve the interests of the elite.

In reflecting on the rule of elite White men in college sport today and into the future, it is important to mention some historical points of reference. First, with its origins in Ivy League institutions (particularly Harvard and Yale) in the mid-1800s, college sport has historically been overwhelmingly shaped by and for elite White males.[25] The crew race organized by White male students at Harvard and Yale in 1852 is widely recognized as the first official intercollegiate athletics event. However, the first recorded American football game between Princeton and Rutgers in 1869 really set the tone for the growth and popularity of college sport, particularly college football, on HWCU campuses.

In a chapter on racial barriers in Eurocentric sport organizations in the book *Systemic Racism*, Anthony Weems and I argue that the creation and expansion of American football in these elite HWCU was largely a social and cultural response to a perceived threat to White masculinity. In the aftermath of significant historical events (such as the abolishment of chattel slavery) that challenged the rule of White male elites, football became one mechanism through which White males would continue reinventing and redefining what it meant to dominate and to exert one's manhood.[26] With the exception of a few talented non-White athletes like William H. Lewis and Jim Thorpe, participation in college football was almost exclusively limited to White men during the late nineteenth century into the early twentieth century. Although football faced potential banishment early on because of its brutal and violent nature, President Theodore Roosevelt intervened by inviting coaches and athletic advisers to the White House to discuss ways to improve the game and make it safer. President Woodrow Wilson would also come to the defense of football. Like Roosevelt, he associated participation in the sport with authentic manhood. The support of these two US Presidents in the first two decades of the twentieth century not only helped quell the calls for football's banishment, but more importantly, contributed greatly to the rapid spread of football to other HWCU and eventually youth sport and the professional ranks.

The second noteworthy historical point of reference I want to mention is the creation of the NCAA in 1906 and its evolution into the predominant governing body for college sport. Originally known as the Intercollegiate Athletic Association of the United States until the name change in 1910, the NCAA was born out of meetings between White male leaders from several HWCU who had assembled to initiate changes in football playing rules. However, it was not until the 1920s that the NCAA began to conduct championships in different sports, beginning with track and field, and later basketball, which would eventually grow into the spectacle and cash cow it has become. As college sport continued to grow in scope and popularity, issues of corruption around athlete recruitment, eligibility, and financial aid led the NCAA to establish the "sanity code" in the late 1940s to address such ethical matters. Meant to prevent the awarding of financial aid to athletes based solely on their athletic prowess, the sanity code required institutions to consider the financial needs and academic accomplishments of prospective athletes. Critics argued that it favored the elite colleges that got the better students and had wealthier alumni who could financially support athletic programs.[27]

The limited effect of this code led to its demise, and the growing commercialism in college sport would eventually lead the NCAA to hire Walter Byers as its first full-time executive director in 1951 and establish a national office in 1952. Byers, who retired in 1987, was arguably the key architect of big-time college sport as we have come to know it in the twenty-first century. In his 1995 memoir, *Unsportsmanlike Conduct*, he exposed the history of corruption and hypocrisy in the NCAA and discussed the flagrant exploitation of athletes in the high-dollar, commercialized college sport marketplace. Byers openly discussed how the NCAA had intentionally introduced the term *student-athlete* to counter the idea that college athletes were employees of its member institutions, and prevent them from being able to claim workers' compensation and other benefits that employees like coaches and other athletic department stakeholders enjoy.[28]

Byers has been criticized for not really owning up to the prominent role he played in establishing the myth of amateurism and the oppressive structures and rules of the NCAA that have continued to grow and persist well into the second decade of the twenty-first century.[29] Significantly, Byers's eventual acknowledgment that a neoplantation mentality and undemocratic form of governance exists in college sport confirmed what Harry Edwards had long asserted when Byers was still executive director of the NCAA.

A critical study and reflection on the history of college sport and the NCAA should prompt us to position and assess powerful White men like Walter Byers and those elite White men who control the levers of power within college sport in the present. To Feagin and Ducey's point, there is a need to call out and directly address how elite White males' myriad concrete society-shaping actions have created and contributed to educational challenges and problems faced by Black male athletes and their peers on the campuses of these HWCU in particular.

Before I end this introduction, I want to offer an important caveat. In discussing the elite White male dominance system, my purpose is not to personally attack or disparage individual White men or the White race as a whole. White people too are genuinely concerned about racial and other forms of social justice, and work to address societal ills related to the systemic racism, systemic sexism, and systemic classism that undergirds the elite White male dominance system. But I also want to make clear that this book is not written to pacify or placate elite or other Whites who remain unaware of or comfortable in their privilege and complacent or complicit in what education scholar David Stovall calls this "political, economic and cultural system in which Whites overwhelmingly control power and material resources, conscious and unconscious ideas of White superiority and entitlement are widespread, and relations of White dominance and non-White subordination are daily reenacted across a broad array of institutions and social settings"[30]; or as philosopher Tommy Curry puts it, this "capitalist ethno-patriarchal regime we call white supremacy."[31]

AN OVERVIEW OF THIS BOOK

This book is divided into four chapters. In chapter 1, I contextualize the significance of studying Black male college athletes, and how their race, gender, and participation in Division I college sport at HWCU impacts their education. More precisely, I discuss the sociopolitical and sociocultural backdrops in which this book came to fruition and how some of my personal and professional experiences inspired my writing as we transitioned from the Obama era into the Trump era. I further elucidate why I focused specifically on Black males and the context of college sport, and discuss the potential educative value of college sport participation.

Chapter 2 presents an instrumental case study of three Black male athletes who were key players and teammates in a highly visible and successful football program at a major HWCU when they initially participated in this study. The chapter highlights their observations on education, the benefits and detriments of college sport participation, matters related to racism, and matters related to institutional integrity. This chapter's focus on these Black males' perspectives on these education matters while they were still college athletes—and several years after their playing days ended—is what makes it so intriguing.

In chapter 3, I draw from data I collected in 2017 and 2018, including written narratives and/or formal individual interviews with nine former Black male football athletes from diverse backgrounds and Division I HWCU across different conferences. I apply the storytelling and experiential knowledge tenets of CRT to present robust case vignettes about these athletes' personal backgrounds and P–12 educational experiences, how they navigated the often difficult and sometimes contradictory educational terrain of college sport, educational and life outcomes related to their college sport participation, and recommendations these Black males offered for improving the relationship between Black males' college sport participation and their education.

I conclude this book in chapter 4 with a brief discussion of macro-, meso-, and micro-level matters related to Black male athletes' education. I imply that people from various racial backgrounds, including White males, who are genuinely concerned about the education of Black male college athletes and their athlete peers should form or become part of cross-race coalitions and use such alliances to combat oppressive forces of this elite White male dominance system in college sport. I end the chapter by advancing some ideas for future research, policy considerations, and recommendations for practices in organized school sport in both higher education and secondary education.

CHAPTER 1

Contextualizing the Significance of Studying Black Male College Athletes

[A]s an educator, my interests were drawn to the political role of education in the larger scheme of oppression of Blacks in America. I have come to understand what people in power have long known—education can be used both to oppress and to liberate.

William Watkins[1]

Unfortunately, African people in the United States still have some prevailing misperceptions about their education and education in general. We were not brought to the United States or the so-called New World to be educated. We were brought as a massive labor supply . . . What the slave masters permitted was training and not education.

John Henrik Clarke[2]

The system of intercollegiate athletics has remained relatively consistent with other social institutions where the Black body is a valued commodity: a cog or a tool for capitalist expansion. Within the context of intercollegiate athletics, the faces and voices change periodically, yet the goal of capital accumulation remains the same.

Billy Hawkins[3]

T O SET THE TONE for and contextualize the significance of my study of Black male college athletes, I took education scholar Rich Milner's advice—that when examining matters of race and culture, we should explicitly position ourselves as researchers.[4] I thus start by introducing three interrelated sources of inspiration for this book: Cornel West's work on race matters; the work of Gloria Ladson-Billings and William Tate,

among others, on critical race theory (CRT) in education; and Tyrone Howard's book *Black Male(d)*, which interrogates and challenges the disenfranchisement of Black males in P–12 schools. I next discuss my journey to
writing this book. Then I discuss why and how Black male college athletes'
race and gender matter and make a case for the continued focus on Black
male football and basketball athletes at HWCU. I end the chapter by raising
and briefly discussing important questions about college sport's legitimacy
in the education of Black male football and basketball athletes.

POSITIONING MYSELF IN THE STUDY OF BLACK MALE
COLLEGE ATHLETES

The first of three major sources of inspiration for this book was Cornel
West's influential book *Race Matters*, which I encountered toward the
end of my undergraduate studies in the mid-1990s. I was deeply struck by
West's observation, "[My wife and I] talked about what *race matters* have
meant to the American past and how much *race matters* in the American
present."[5] For me, *race matters* involve the salient issues that have emerged
particularly for Black and other non-White people with the social and legal
construction of race by White men (i.e., European colonizers) in the US.
The creation of racial categories and hierarchies by these colonizers was
rooted in a White supremacist mind-set, and this helps explain why and
how a system of institutionalized racism—where Whites have deemed
themselves to be superior to all other racial groups and entitled to certain
rights and privileges that racialized others were not—became endemic in
US society in particular. In addition, *race matters* also speak to the great
significance and influence of race, and how it operates (often in complex
and fluid ways) in various US social institutions and cultural practices. I
have come to learn that education and sport are prominent examples of
social and cultural contexts where race does indeed matter, and matters
pertaining to race continue to infiltrate and play a significant role in these
intertwined contexts.

Second and related to West's work, is the interrogation of the centrality of race and racism in the field of education. I was exposed as a doctoral student to the work of Gloria Ladson-Billings and William Tate, who
have been credited with formally introducing *critical race theory* (CRT)
to the field in the mid-to-late 1990s.[6] This germinal work provided other

education scholars with valuable analytic and explanatory tools to better understand and address various race matters that affect students of color in particular during the first decades of the twenty-first century.[7]

Third, Tyrone Howard's application of CRT in his book *Black Male(d)* is particularly noteworthy and relevant to this book. Howard draws from CRT to focus on the disenfranchisement of Black males in P–12 schools. He specifically devotes a chapter to a discussion of the athletic/academic paradigm and Black males' place within it. Howard coins the term *athlete seasoning complex* to describe a process whereby young Black boys—from as early as four or five years old—are encouraged by family and influential others to focus intensely and persistently on developing high proficiency in sports with the goal of achieving social mobility at the college and professional sport levels.[8] Unfortunately, for many of these young Black males, this pursuit of excellence in sport comes at the expense of academic and other areas of meaningful development.

As will be discussed further in this chapter, college sport is at the heart of the athlete seasoning complex. In light of many young Black males' overly time-consuming pursuit of excellence in (especially) football and basketball from early elementary school through higher education, Howard, like others before him, questions how constructive participation in these sports is or has been for the education of Black males. This is a question I also address in this book. However, while I do provide some insight into how Black male athletes' P–12 schooling and upbringing helped influenced their education as college athletes, I was particularly interested in addressing how college sport participation influenced these Black males during their time on campus and after their playing careers ended.

MY JOURNEY TO THIS PROJECT

Before I address the central question of this book—*What does college sport have to do with the education of Black male athletes?*—it is important to provide insight into its historical origins. My scholarly interest in Black male college athletes was conceived in the mid-to-late 1990s, in the midst of noteworthy social, political, economic, and cultural events and developments in the US. One of the most impactful was the historic 1995 Million Man March (MMM), a powerful effort to politically mobilize and galvanize Black males from various walks of life to take personal responsibility for

improving themselves and their communities in a society that has exhibited anti-Black racism and misandry toward Black males from its very
inception. And despite criticisms and efforts from Whites, and even some
Blacks, to undermine the significance of the MMM, this peaceful gathering
of Black men, boys, women, and girls on the Washington, DC Mall served
as an important counter-narrative to the negative stereotypes and portray-
als of Black males throughout US history. I was unable to attend the march,
but this purposeful gathering of Black males planted a seed.

The MMM took place in late October just days after the "not guilty"
verdict was announced in the racially charged and polarizing murder trial
of O. J. Simpson. At one time, Simpson had been beloved by the White
mainstream, first as a star college and professional football running back in
the 1960s and 1970s, and then in his post-playing career doing major television commercials, sports broadcasting, and acting. But now, Simpson's
acquittal of the murders of his former wife (a White woman) and her friend
(a White male) further inflamed racial tensions that still lingered from the
1992 Los Angeles riots that had broken out in the aftermath of the acquittal
of four White police officers who were captured on video brutally beating
Black motorist Rodney King. The riots laid bare the deep racial divide that
has long existed between Blacks and Whites in particular.

At the time, I was a fifth-year senior at Michigan State University
(MSU). I vividly remember my Black roommate (who was a starter and key
player on the men's basketball team) and I watching the O. J. Simpson verdict on that early October day with several other tenants, who were mostly
White, in the common area of the apartment complex we lived in. Both
my roommate and I seemed to be pleased or at least okay with the verdict,
even if we were unsure about his innocence or guilt. On the other hand, the
majority of the White viewers were visibly and vocally disappointed in it.
This division was consistent with general attitudes Blacks and Whites held
toward the verdict across the country. Whites generally seemed to believe
Simpson was guilty of murder and were enraged by his acquittal. Blacks,
whether they thought he was guilty or not, tended to view his acquittal as a
form of symbolic justice for the long history of physical and psychological
violence Blacks have experienced at the hands of Whites and the criminal
justice and other US social systems White people have created.

In the years following the MMM and my undergraduate studies, critical conversations I had with my eighteen-months-younger brother, Marcus,

about the plight of Black people, particularly Black males, in the US helped ignite my interest in the study of race and gender matters related to Black male athletes' education. Since our days growing up in Niles and Benton Harbor, Michigan, playing on the same youth baseball teams, and later, high school varsity basketball team, we have always been close friends. However, in 1996, during his senior year as a Division I basketball player at DePaul University, a HWCU with a storied program history, my baby brother had made the controversial and unpopular decision to join the Nation of Islam (NOI) and become a practicing Muslim. This bold decision eventually drew us even closer together. His spiritual and religious conversion to Islam (we were born and raised in the Christian church) initially shook and troubled me. But it challenged me to come to grips with his profound transformation and what that meant for our relationship and his life journey going forward. It forced me to begin learning more about the history of Black people in the US and throughout the world. I became more interested in seeking greater knowledge of self and my purpose in life as a Black man in America. Many of the points I raise in this book grew from conversations Marcus and I have had about race, sport, and education.

I returned to MSU for graduate school in 1997 armed with a strong inclination to pursue knowledge about Black experiences in US society. I began to read, study, and engage more in conversations and debates about the plight of Black people with some of my peers. I took an elective course in sociocultural issues in sport, taught by sport sociologist Yevonne Smith, which played an important role in heightening my interest in the intersections between race, sport, and education. However, it was my graduate assistantship for the Summer University Program Excellence Required (SUPER) program at MSU that really propelled me into the informal and formal study of Black male athletes' education matters. This summer bridge program was designed to help transition supposedly at-risk, mostly racial minority students, including football and basketball athletes, from high school into their first year at the university. My observations and interactions with the coaches, administrators, and academic counselors, among others, and the wonderful Black male athletes who came through the program over the course of my three summers with SUPER prompted me to begin asking critical questions about the NCAA and college sport and the organizational cultures, structures, policies, practices, processes, and personnel in athletic departments at HWCU.

This initial foray into the critical study of Black male athletes' education is what guided my decision to pursue doctoral studies in sport management at Ohio State University (OSU) and develop a research agenda around race, sport, and education.

However, the idea and vision for this book did not begin to take shape until late 2009. In November of that year, I was invited by Mary Shaw, the director of the Center for the Study of Health Disparities in the Department of Health and Kinesiology (HLKN) at Texas A&M University (TAMU) to give a talk designed to promote interdisciplinary research and dialogue within the department and beyond. I chose to explore and position the broad topic—"The Mis-education of Black Male College Athletes"—as an important social and public health matter scholars might examine from diverse disciplinary angles. From that point forward, I gave a series of formal lectures and talks on this complex topic to audiences at HWCU, academic conferences, and in K–12 school districts. I drew inspiration from historian Carter G. Woodson's timeless books *The Education of the Negro* and *The Mis-Education of the Negro*, from principles of CRT, and some of my earlier research and practical experiences with Black male college athletes to explore pertinent multifaceted forces that unduly affect the education of Black male college athletes at HWCU.[9] I received positive and constructive feedback from friends, colleagues, and strangers alike. This feedback, and the encouragement some gave me to organize my thoughts into a book, persuaded me that I should pursue this project, with the above-mentioned talks forming the basis for much of my conceptual thinking and framing of the book.

My conceptualization gained momentum and became more lucid a few years after the controversial Black Lives Matter (BLM) movement was formally inspired by three Black women in 2013 as a rallying cry against the racial profiling and police brutality that continues to be directed toward Black males in particular.[10] Despite heavy criticism from many Whites (as well as some Blacks and other non-Whites), this movement has shown potential to serve as a mechanism of resistance and pushback against the blatant disregard for and devaluation of Black life that continues to pervade US society. Many White critics in particular like to point to the election and reelection of Barack Obama, the first Black president in US history, to justify their often misguided anti-BLM sentiments.[11] There is widespread belief among many that Obama's political rise demonstrates the US has resolved its deeply racist past, and moved toward a colorblind and post-racial society where race no longer really matters and has no bearing on life opportunities and outcomes Black and other non-White people experience. Black males' continued and heightened visibility and prominence as college and professional athletes has certainly contributed to this embrace of such narratives. Many critics of BLM point to the social status and luxurious lifestyles of Black male professional athletes and Black people in other professions outside of sports to suggest that Black people today are actually privileged, and thus, there is no need for a BLM movement

I find such post-racial and colorblind narratives to be nonsensical and incredibly dishonest because they focus primarily on the upward social mobility of a few Black people but largely ignore the realities of countless others who struggle every day to navigate the elite White male dominance system, particularly during and since our transition from the Obama to Trump era. The events that have occurred in the aftermath of President Obama's time in office are strong indicators of the ever-increasing, not a declining, significance of race as has been suggested in the past by some scholars and social commentators.[12] To be sure, it is not uncommon for US presidents to be subject to criticism by people who are opposed to their actions, policies, or mere presence in office. As with any other president, some criticisms leveled against President Obama were/are perhaps legitimate. However, the contemptible treatment of Obama during his presidency and the utter disrespect and racial hostility directed toward President Obama and his family (particularly by Whites) is unprecedented, and ugly proof that race still very much matters.

The election of Donald Trump as Obama's successor speaks volumes about the troubling state of race relations in US society. Trump—described by Cornel West as the personification of "White male mediocrity and mendacity"[13]—is an extremely polarizing figure who capitalized on the "birther" lie in efforts to undermine the legitimacy of President Obama and his US citizenship. Trump's ascension to the White House represents a blatant continuation of the long legacy of White male patriarchy and privilege in the US, and a virulent form of White resentment and backlash against the racial progress Obama symbolized. Trump's disastrous and destructive presidency is essentially the manifestation of what the US has always been, but racial and other forms of social injustice have been visibly exacerbated on his watch. Trump in many ways can be considered the perfect mascot for White supremacy because he is a flamboyant character who essentially serves as a mouthpiece and instrument for the celebration, amplification, and continuation of elite White male dominance in US society. His candidacy and presidency have helped renew, reinforce, and further expose the White supremacist ideology, racism, sexism, xenophobia, and religious intolerance that has plagued US society and intergroup relations for centuries. Not only do racism and other forms of covert discrimination continue to permeate US social institutions, including education and sport, but Whites from various backgrounds have also been emboldened to express overtly bigoted attitudes and sometimes violent behaviors toward various non-White groups and individuals perceived to be enemies or outsiders.

These attitudes directly touch Black male athletes. Many have been categorized as such enemies or outsiders, particularly those who have dared to use their platform to speak up and act out against racial and other forms of social injustice. Perhaps the most well-known example today is Colin Kaepernick's decision in 2016 to take a knee during the national anthem. Kaepernick's protest against police brutality and other forms of state violence against Black people subjected him to both covert (e.g., NFL owners seemingly colluding to blackball him from the league) and overt (e.g., death threats, burning his jersey) racism. Kaepernick's courageous stand in the face of this negative backlash helped define what Harry Edwards has called the *fourth wave* or era of athlete activism.[14] It has inspired other professional, college, and even high school and youth sport athletes to use their platforms to speak up and act out against social injustice via social media and other mediums. In his timely book *Things That Make White People Uncomfortable*, Super Bowl Champion and three-time All-Pro defensive end Michael Bennett discussed his brotherhood with Kaepernick and other NFL players and shared some of the negative backlash he and his NFL peers, particularly Black players, experienced as a result of their activism.[15] Amazingly, some of this backlash included being verbally attacked and vilified by President Trump himself, who referred to players who kneel as "sons of bitches." Instances such as this one prompted Bennett, during an interview he did on the topic of education matters with Etan Thomas, to remind his fellow Black male athletes "that we are still Black men living in this society, and the struggle is real."[16]

In the chapter entitled, "The NCAA Will Give You PTSD," Bennett directly addresses the experience of Black male college athletes. He discusses his educational experiences as a Division I college football athlete and the challenges his Black teammates and he faced in grappling with oppressive NCAA policies while navigating the racially hostile environment of the college town, HWCU, and athletic program they were in. Recognizing the collective power college athletes (past and present) have but often fail to realize during their playing days, Bennett reflects, "If I had it to do over, I would have tried to flex that power." He points to the University of Missouri football players' protest against racism on their campus in 2015 as an example of this collective power. As a Black male scholar and educator who embraces an athletes' rights approach to college sport reform, I was fascinated by the stand these Black (and some White) male athletes took in support of their fellow non-athlete peers at the university.[17] It makes me reflect on the sentiments of historian John Henrik Clarke, who suggested that one true purpose of education is to prepare students to understand and handle power responsibly.[18] It certainly appears the University of Missouri football players understood and used their collective power responsibly in threatening not to play in an upcoming Saturday football game if the university failed to take action to address the racial injustice Black students faced on campus. The social activism exhibited by these college athletes contradicts research that suggests there is a disconnect between the values of civic responsibility that high-profile college athletes profess and their ability to translate these social values into social action.[19] The Missouri football players' decision to create and take advantage of the opportunity to directly address racism in their educational environment is a prime example of educational empowerment.

Although this book is not specifically about college athlete activism per se, the topic is certainly relevant to the discussion of Black male athlete education matters, and did come up in my interviews and conversations with some of the Black male athletes who are featured in chapters 2 and 3 of this book. In this regard, the topic of athlete activism is an important education matter to consider going forward.

WHY BLACK MALE ATHLETES?

Before elaborating on why I emphasize the study of and with Black male athletes, I need to acknowledge that they are not a monolithic group. These athletes represent a wide range of individuals who bring diverse attributes, educational backgrounds and learning needs, and complex identities to college campuses. Black male college athletes from P–12 public schools in high-poverty urban or rural areas and those from private schools in middle- to upper-middle-class suburban areas will have had different experiences because of their socioeconomic and social class status. Moreover, their experiences can be further complicated because of their religious affiliation (e.g., Muslim), sexual identity (e.g., gay), family structure (e.g., single-parent upbringing), or parental status (e.g., father of one or more children). Finally, male athletes who might by social norms be considered "Black" but were born and raised outside the US or view themselves as biracial, multiracial, or not Black at all might bring different lived experiences, perspectives, interests, commitments, and needs to HWCU and their athletic programs. And as with any group, Black male college athletes with similar demographic backgrounds and experiences are separate individuals who could view the world very differently. In other words, the vast intragroup diversity among Black male college athletes should be taken into account when studying matters related to their education.

In this book, I use the term *Black male athletes* in making reference to this particular college student group in a broad sense. Clearly, the members of this highly diverse student group do not speak with a single voice or experience the world in the same manner. That said, despite their different experiences, Black male athletes may face similar challenges because of their race, gender, and/or athletic identity. I agree with education and CRT scholars Adrienne Dixson and Celia Rousseau, who also point out that the personal narratives and stories of students of color might be different and contend, "Although there is not one common voice, there is a common experience of racism that structures the stories of people of colour and allows for the use of the term voice."[20] As I highlighted in the introduction, Black male athletes in the US live, attend schools, and play sports in a society and educational system that is rooted in the elite White male dominance system, and this reality constantly threatens to undermine their education and negatively impact their holistic development in myriad ways some of them might not even be aware of, care about, believe, or accept. The personal narratives of the twelve Black male athletes featured in this book suggest this group had at least some awareness of the elite White male dominance system and the challenges it presented to their education.

Building on the arguments I made in the introduction, the fundamental reason I chose to focus specifically on Black male athletes in this book is because, throughout history, being Black and male (athlete or not) in this White man's world has far too often been detrimental to the life experiences and outcomes of this particular social group. This point has been well documented over the course of decades. In *The Assassination of the Black Male Image*, Earl Ofari Hutchinson discussed White Americans' disdain for Black males' very being and existence, but interest in the manipulation and exploitation of their physical attributes and prowess, a point that directly relates to Black male athletes today and I will discuss below. According to Hutchinson,

> Many Americans hate and fear black men. Yet they are fascinated with them. *They love to see them sing, dance, lug, and toss those balls.* In deeply sexist America, the game is still about white male ego, power, and control. Black men are perceived as threats to all . . . the privileged and wealthy men that call the shots in America don't need to wage the same ego war against black women as they do against black men."[21]

In their book *Black Man Emerging*, psychologists Joseph White and James Cones III support Hutchinson's point about the perception of Black males as America's villains and the greatest threat to their White male counterparts. These authors argue, "The intensely negative view of Black men has far surpassed the disfavor in which other oppressed peoples are held." They examine "the dismal sociological and economic conditions of life in America that many Black males encounter as they make their passage from cradle to grave."[22] Ellis Cose's book *The Envy of the World* further argues that the world sets Black males "apart from normal humanity" and Black males' very existence evokes certain feelings of "envy and loathing."[23]

More recently, in his book, *The Man-Not*, philosopher Tommy Curry invokes the term *Black male vulnerability* to describe the disadvantages Black males endure in comparison with other groups; the erasure of their lived experience from theory; and the violence and death they constantly suffer in society. In challenging some of the contemporary theories of gender hierarchy, Curry further argues that Black male vulnerability extends well beyond the material disadvantages Black males face:

The term is also meant to express the vulnerable condition—the sheer fungibility—of the Black male as a living terror able to be killed, raped, or dehumanized at any given moment, given the disposition of those who encounter him. Black male vulnerability is an attempt to capture the Black male's perpetual susceptibility to the will of others, how he has no resistance to the imposition of others' fears and anxieties on him. Despite the contemporary intersectional, feminist, and liberal-progressive framings of gender hierarchies that maintain Black men have some privilege based on their maleness, Black men and boys lag behind on practically every population indicator, from education and income to health and mortality.[24]

Curry's claims are supported by data that reveal that Black males are more likely to be homicide victims, unemployed or underemployed, incarcerated, on parole or probation, out on bond, or being sought on warrant by law enforcement. They have shorter life expectancies and are more likely to have debilitating medical problems and poor occupational training, among other problems. Such disturbing data provide strong support for scholar Wesley Muhammad's argument that there has long been an assault on Black males.[25] This assault is precisely why, as suggested by Curry, we should center Black male studies and create robust theories around the Black male experience.

This Black male studies agenda should include a continued and more nuanced focus on Black male college athletes because, as Hutchinson's work cited above suggests, on the one hand, many Americans have exhibited great disdain toward Black males and viewed them as the ultimate threat and menace to society. But on the other hand, they have seemed (at least on the surface) to love seeing Black males engage in sport and play as great football and basketball athletes for HWCU and American professional sport teams. In fact, some people—including Black male athletes themselves—believe sport is "one of the few places where an African American man can be a man."[26] That is, the fields and courts of play is one of the few contexts where Black males are valued and respected, and their lives seemingly matter.

It is also a commonly held belief that Black male football and basketball athletes at HWCU enjoy certain privileges that their female counterparts—and for that matter, even some of their White male counterparts from sports outside of football and basketball—do not. I acknowledge that Black male athletes (and many of their peers) do enjoy tangible and intangible benefits; for example, athletic scholarships, travel opportunities, access to academic support and life skills services, access to expert coaching and state-of-the-art playing and training facilities, a major platform to showcase athletic skills, social networks and lifelong friendships, and exposure to people from diverse backgrounds might all be considered valuable benefits. However, I argue that receiving such benefits does not necessarily empower or shield athletes from the detrimental impact some of the NCAA's and its member institutions' oppressive policies and practices often have on the education of college athletes in general, and Black male athletes in particular.

CHALLENGES FACING BLACK MALE ATHLETES IN HIGHER EDUCATION

In further discussing why it is necessary to centralize the study of Black male college athletes, it is important to account for the challenges Black males in general have grappled with as students in the broader US educational system. Tyrone Howard and other education scholars have documented how Black males in the P–12 context are at the very bottom of a socially constructed hierarchy with respect to educational attainment and almost every indicator of academic performance and success, including GPA, standardized test scores, and graduation rates. Furthermore, in comparison to their peers, Black males are typically the most severely and disproportionately affected by the P–12 schooling process. They consistently have higher suspension and expulsion rates; higher dropout rates; overrepresentation in special education, remedial courses, and alternative learning environments; and underrepresentation in honors courses, gifted programs, and Advanced Placement.[27] Black males in higher education have also faced significant challenges and barriers. For example, with the exception of historically Black colleges and universities (HBCU), Black males have had limited access to institutions of higher education. Moreover, the graduation rates of those relative few who do enroll at HWCU have been dismal in comparison to their peers at these institutions.

Yet, as I noted in the introduction, since the 1970s, these institutions have made an exception for and demonstrated a strong commitment to providing athletically gifted Black males access to campus via their football, basketball, and increasingly, track and field programs. This is an example of CRT pioneer Derrick Bell's *interest-convergence principle*, which posits that White elites will tolerate or support the advancement of racial minorities only or particularly when it promotes their own interests.[28] Since O. J. Simpson won his Heisman Trophy as a running back at the University of Southern California (USC) in 1968, and two years later, Sam "Bam" Cunningham—another talented Black running back for USC—turned in a dominant performance in a victory against legendary Alabama coach Bear Bryant's all-White squad, HWCU have routinely and aggressively recruited Black males to populate and play predominant roles in their football and basketball programs. (The Racial and Gender Report Cards [RGRC] for college sport developed by Richard Lapchick and colleagues reveal that Black males have been the majority of football and basketball athletes, particularly in the skill positions—for example, running back, wide receiver, defensive backs, and kick and punt returners—at Division I HWCU since at least the early part of the 2000s.) These programs serve as the economic engine that supports the budget of other athletic programs and the overall athletic department.[29] I would argue that Black male football and basketball athletes have emerged as the primary breadwinner for athletic departments at many major HWCU. They have indeed become that "massive labor supply" of John Henrik Clarke's quote at the beginning of this chapter.

However, Black males continue to be conspicuously missing from the general student body, particularly at those HWCU whose athletic departments have the highest national visibility and largest operating budgets. According to the 2016 *Black Male Student-Athletes and Racial Inequities in Division I College Sports* report, within the sixty-five NCAA institutions representing the top five athletic conferences, Black males represented 56.3 percent of the football teams and 60.8 percent of the men's basketball teams during the 2014–2015 academic year, but only 2.5 percent of the undergraduate students.[30] Such data suggest these HWCU are much more interested in Black males' athletic prowess than they are any other potential or talents Black males could bring to the student body as non-athletes. In D. Stanley Eitzen's words, this practice of over-recruiting Black males for their athletic abilities and under-recruiting them for their academic and other abilities "reinforces the negative stereotype that African Americans are endowed with special physical attributes but lack the necessary mental attributes" to contribute something of value beyond their athletic prowess to the student bodies at these institutions.[31]

The irony is that although Black males with academic and other abilities are excluded from HWCU that seek similar attributes in White students, these institutions aggressively recruit Black male athletes from secondary schools and offer them full-ride athletic scholarships even when the P–12 academic preparation and backgrounds of some would almost certainly preclude them from admission otherwise. These athletes are referred to as *special admits*. The prevalence of Black male football and basketball athletes who are special admits at HWCU explains, at least in part, why this group is the least prepared academically in comparison with other student groups transitioning from secondary to higher education.

Once they are on campus, Black male football and basketball athletes have typically been at the bottom of most measures of academic success, including GPA and graduation rates. They often spend inordinate amounts of time on athletic activities—including physically and mentally grueling practices and workouts, film study, team meetings, and travel to and from games—in comparison with other developmentally useful activities outside of sport participation. They are often isolated, both voluntarily and involuntarily, from the general student body and other important people on campus. Perhaps most detrimentally, this isolation from faculty of color could deprive them of important mentoring and learning opportunities.[32] Furthermore, they are often clustered into courses and academic majors that do not necessarily serve their educational interests and needs.[33] And those Black male athletes who have a high-profile existence on campus are sometimes disadvantaged because they must deal with the added pressures and public scrutiny that comes with it.

The demanding and often competing expectations associated with being labeled a "student-athlete" on these campuses today sometimes makes it difficult for Black male athletes—even those who do come to campus with strong academic profiles and student identities—to embrace the student role. As sociologists Patricia and Peter Adler found in their longitudinal ethnographic research, these athletes might still struggle academically and become engulfed in the athlete role.[34] Despite the abundant attention Black male college athletes have received over the decades from scholars, educators, the media, and other interested parties, their disenfranchisement persists and, I would argue, has gotten worse under the academic capitalist model that has come to define and permeate higher education in general and college sport governance in particular. In *Sport and the Neoliberal University*, Ryan King-White discusses how the emergence in the 1970s of neoliberalism as a political-economic governing formation has created an educational environment and administrative structure in higher education that is more akin to a private enterprise.[35] Education as the primary function of the college/university has taken a back seat to the commercial interests of the powerful elites, and this has had an especially deleterious impact on Black male athletes. Thus, the education of Black male athletes (and their peers) warrants our attention more now than ever before.

P-12 SCHOOLING AND THE CONVEYOR BELT

I have often heard people say, "it is too late" if you wait until Black male athletes arrive on a college or university campus to address matters related to their education. Although I choose not to use such language or frame it in that manner, I do understand that many of the challenges some Black male athletes face as students in higher education often originate well before they reach higher education. Scholars have acknowledged the impact of out-of-school factors—including socioeconomic status, peer influence, mental health, parental involvement and support, and neighborhood environments—on Black males' development and life outcomes. However, the role of the P–12 schooling process cannot be understated. As Pedro Noguera states in his book *The Trouble with Black Boys*, "The pressures, stereotypes, and patterns of failure that Black males experience often begin in school."[36] Unfortunately, these factors are often more pronounced for some Black males who play organized school sport.

As mentioned earlier in this chapter, many Black males who demonstrate athletic prowess at an early age develop strong athletic identities and lose interest in academic and other non-sport-related identities and educational activities in and out of school. This reality is often magnified for Black males who have shown potential to play college sport as they move from elementary into secondary school on what journalist William Rhoden referred to as the "conveyor belt" in his book *Forty Million Dollar Slaves*.[37] Essentially, this term refers to the recruiting apparatus or process that extracts talented Black athletes from their communities (often urban and rural) and depending on their athletic prowess moves them up and through the different levels of the sport hierarchy—youth to professional—while socializing them to think and comport themselves in a manner that largely allows the exploitative system to remain intact. In other words, the allure of the belt and the potential for fame and fortune for the few who make it to the end often discourages Black male athletes from critically examining the system and its exploitive nature.

The story of former high school football standout Derek Sparks in the book *Lessons of the Game* provides a vivid example of the exploitative nature of the conveyor belt. This story reveals how coaches, administrators, family members, and other stakeholders socialized a young Black male athlete who grew up in poverty to engage in behaviors that restricted his academic and personal development. In particular, Sparks's transfer to four different high schools in four different years speaks to the great lengths he went in pursuit of upward social mobility through football.[38] Although injuries throughout his college playing career at Washington State University along with other setbacks in life served as barriers to achieving his dreams of playing in the NFL, Sparks's story is a reminder that Black male athletes who have shown great athletic potential are enticed to remain on and continue along the conveyor belt, with promises of college athletic scholarships for the elite, and professional sport contracts for the elite of the elite.[39]

As a prominent example of how the conveyor belt operates on a macro-level, the big business enterprise of Amateur Athletic Union (AAU) club basketball has in many ways usurped the role of the high school basketball team and become the primary path to college and professional basketball for top players.[40] High school sport still plays an important role in student opportunities and achievement, at least in the sense that athletes are required to maintain academic eligibility and earn a high school diploma to be eligible to play college sport. Thus, as research has shown, participation in high school sport can positively contribute to Black males' academic engagement and outcomes, including attendance, grades, motivation to stay in school, graduation rates, and college attendance.[41]

WHY COLLEGE SPORT?

I maintain a specific focus in this book on college sport at HWCU for a few reasons. First, college sport is what I am most familiar with, and thus most interested in further studying, critically interrogating, and better understanding. From the time I left home as an almost-eighteen-year old to attend MSU to now, as a forty-five-year old Black male faculty administrator at TAMU, I have been intrigued by the spectacle of college sport and the leading role Black male football and basketball athletes play in it. As an undergraduate student who pursued a walk-on spot on the Division I college basketball team, but in the process, jeopardized my academic scholarship by going on academic probation, I got my first real taste of the powerful lure big-time college sport can have on young Black males. Although I was not even recruited to play at MSU and ended up never playing there, I still was caught up to some extent in the trappings of athletic role engulfment. Since that time, the myriad roles I have played—through my years at MSU as an undergraduate and graduate student, as academic adviser and mentor to college athletes in SUPER, as a doctoral student at OSU, as a faculty member at James Madison University and TAMU, and more recently, as chair of the president's athletics council at TAMU— greatly influenced how I went about writing this book. These personal and professional experiences have allowed me to speak with a certain authority and credibility and lend an important voice and perspective on Black male athlete education matters in and through college sport.

Second, given how and where college sport is positioned within the hierarchy of the US sport industry, I view it as the epicenter or central point of this powerful, multibillion-dollar enterprise. According to B. David Ridpath, college sport was the impetus behind the growth and development of sport programs in primary and secondary levels of US education. It continues to significantly influence how these levels below it operate and function. Interscholastic sport programs, particularly football and basketball, have adopted elements of the academic capitalist model that undergirds college sport. With a strong emphasis on business concerns and the financial bottom line, the academic capitalist model in many ways mirrors the professional sport business model. In fact, there is an inextricable link between college and professional sport, particularly because the former serves as the primary feeder system for the latter. Professional sport leagues, particularly the NFL and NBA, rely heavily on NCAA Division I institutions to further develop (at little to no cost) the talent and brands of college athletes before they permit them to become officially eligible to enter these leagues via their annual drafts.

It must be noted, however, that there are other ways that high school football and basketball athletes can enter the professional sport system. They can technically choose to skip college and pursue professional playing careers internationally (particularly in basketball) or train on their own until they become eligible for the NFL and NBA drafts. More recently though, the G-League, the developmental or minor league for the NBA, has created an option for top prospects to bypass college all together. In addition, at the time I finished writing this book, NBA commissioner, Adam Silver had proposed lowering the NBA draft-eligible age limit from nineteen to eighteen years old. If approved, this proposal would essentially allow high school basketball athletes—beginning with the 2022 NBA draft—to go directly from high school to the NBA without having to spend a year playing college basketball.[42] Despite this, US college sport is typically still the most viable path to these leagues for the overwhelming majority of aspiring professional athletes in the US

Finally, essentially from the very beginning of college sport, various groups and individuals have argued that college sport is highly corrupt and antithetical to higher education. In the provocative book *Air Ball* John Gerdy argues that institutions of higher education should get out of the entertainment business of big-time college sport because this experiment with elite athletics has failed to address the educational and public health needs of our citizens. Gerdy and others have presented compelling arguments against the professionalization of college sport and offered proposals for alternative models.[43] However, the professionalization and hyper-commercialism in college sport only continues to grow, and scandals and corruption continue to make headlines (e.g., the FBI probe into the college basketball recruiting and bribery scandal that first surfaced in September 2017).

Football and basketball programs at HWCU still hold deep meaning for the coaches, administrators, support staff, student body, college athletes within institutions of higher education and the fans, alumni, boosters, corporate sponsors, media, the NCAA headquarters, professional sport leagues outside them. In an article on the cultural significance of US college sport, Janice Beyer and David Hannah suggest that meaningful and substantial reform will be extremely difficult to achieve because of college sport's cultural embeddedness in US society and higher education, and the positive functions and benefits powerful groups and people often associate with this cultural phenomenon.[44] Given this reality, the critical study of college sport and Black male athletes' role as the most valuable commodity and instrument for capitalist expansion in this enterprise (see Hawkins's quote at beginning of this chapter) remains a critically important undertaking.

EDUCATION AS A LEGITIMATION OF COLLEGE SPORT?

Sport management and policy scholar Laurence Chalip has discussed central legitimations of sport and how scholars and practitioners can work to optimize the good—and perhaps mitigate the bad—that is produced in and through athletic programs. He argues that a key challenge for those who manage sport organizations and programs is to plan, organize, lead, and evaluate sport in a manner that justifies its existence and the public's investment in it.[45] Essentially, Chalip highlights the need for leaders in sport organizations and programs to demonstrate why sport matters, and how there is a need to view sport as an effective mechanism to address broader societal matters instead of just a commercialized spectacle shaped by marketplace rationality.

Although Chalip did not explicitly focus on education as one of the potential legitimations of sport, scholars and social commentators have debated for decades whether or not (and how) sport contributes to the overall development and well-being of athletes at both the interscholastic and intercollegiate levels. On the one hand, the "sport enhances" thesis argues, for example, that sport participation can greatly improve physical fitness and overall health; help build social networks; nurture teamwork, work ethic, leadership, perseverance, discipline, time management, and other characteristics that are beneficial in the job market and other spheres of social life; and help facilitate behavioral, emotional, cognitive engagement and achievement. On the other hand, advocates for the "sport impedes" thesis assert that sport participation can negatively divert attention away from academic pursuits, encourage anti-intellectualism and an overemphasis on physical skill development, and lead to major injuries and health issues—for example, concussions and other debilitating injuries common in football—that compromise quality of life for participants. As it relates specifically to Black males and college sport, the "sport enhances" perspective suggests that college sport provides Black males (particularly those from underprivileged economic and schooling backgrounds) access to educational and career opportunities that otherwise might not be available to them. The "sport impedes" perspective asserts that the hyper-commercialization of college sport in recent decades has led to the exploitation of Black male athletes' athletic abilities and the degradation of development in academic, intellectual, social, and other areas. Research has supported both these perspectives, and some of the narratives in chapters 2 and 3 support both of these perspectives.

In thinking more deeply about the nexus of higher education and college sport, it always amazes me when I hear people, including students I teach and everyday fans of college sports, say that college athletes have it made because they are getting a "free education" through athletic scholarships or grant in aids at HWCU. I find such claims to be absurd, particularly when you consider the very long hours and the great physical, mental, and emotional energy athletes put into college sport participation. Many of the Black male athletes I have interacted with over the years would tell you that playing college football and/or basketball is akin to having an unpaid full-time job, while still trying to be a full-time college student. The fact that most Black male football and basketball athletes at HWCU do not have to pay tuition, student fees, or for books, and that they receive perks such as small monthly stipends, athletic apparel, and meal plans, should not be equated to or confused with receiving a "free education." When you take into account that the overwhelming majority of these athletes are recruited to these HWCU solely because of athletic prowess, the question remains: Are Black male football and basketball athletes afforded real opportunities to pursue meaningful education once they are on campus?

In critically pondering that question, it is important to revisit my brief discussion of education from the introduction. To reiterate, education can be described as the act or process of imparting or acquiring basic (and sometimes advanced) knowledge and understanding of various subject matters and topics of study, developing abilities and powers of reasoning and judgment (i.e., use of knowledge), and preparing oneself or others—intellectually and otherwise—for mature life as well as particular careers or professions.[46] It is a process where the inner gifts, talents, and abilities that an individual possesses are cultivated and drawn out when that individual is exposed to proper teaching and learning environments. In this regard, while learning in a classroom setting is certainly an important aspect of education, it is but one component. As students grow older and mature cognitively, education also involves questioning and reflecting on what is being taught and learned, both inside and outside the classroom. It is about developing an understanding of self, others, and the world; using that knowledge to discover one's purpose; and being set on a path toward fulfilling one's potential and purpose in life. (In chapters 2 and 3, I highlight the definitions of education that were shared by the Black male college athletes I interviewed.)

Given the history and legacy of White supremacy and racism in US society, scholars have long argued the US educational system was not designed to serve the best interests of Black people. This is one of the take-home messages from Carter G. Woodson's *The Mis-Education of the Negro.* Woodson described this system as antiquated and one that distorts the history of Black people. Moreover, he boldly claimed that when Black people finish their formal education in schools, they have been "equipped to begin the life of an Americanized or Europeanized white man."[47] Mwalimu Shujaa echoes Woodson's claims. In his book *Too Much Schooling, Too Little Education,* he suggests that *schooling* for Black people in this racist system involves being trained to acquiesce to the dominant social order, where they frequently adopt the cultural orientations of elite Whites, often to their own detriment. *Education,* on the other hand, is when Black people are in learning environments that recognize their cultural history and heritage, facilitate the transmission of cultural knowledge, and affirm their cultural identity.[48] As William Watkins's quote at the beginning of this chapter suggests, White male power elites have always understood the importance and powerful role of true education in the liberation of Black people, and thus used miseducation as a mechanism to oppress them. In previous work on how this affects Black male college athletes, I have described *miseducation* as "a process that often occurs when one is given a wrong or faulty education and where, oftentimes, external forces restrict or impair students' ability to explore the totality of who they are, what they are, and their options and possibilities in various life domains."[49]

Louis Harrison and colleagues explicitly engage text from Woodson's book to critically examine the miseducation of Black college athletes at

HWCU in contemporary times. More specifically, these scholars focus on how the early childhood sport socialization process and the robust athletic identity that often results are two important constructs to consider in thinking about the education of Black college athletes. They focus on the lack of knowledge or understanding among today's Black athletes of the significant influence and non-sport-related accomplishments of Black scholar athletes from the past; the hidden curriculum; and the influence of media depictions (particularly stereotypes) as examples of "mis-educative influences" in the lives of Black college athletes.[50] Essentially, their work demonstrates how the athletics industrial complex severely restricts or impairs these athletes' ability to fully pursue a deep and meaningful education. According to Harrison and colleagues, a wide opportunity gap exists in the education of Black college athletes at HWCU:

> [Black athletes] are recruited to attend some of the most prestigious institutions of higher learning, yet they often are not afforded the benefit of the vast intellectual resources available in these institutions. They are afforded "scholarships" to attend these universities but are often not privy to the abundant scholarly resources available at these universities due to athletic responsibilities. Ironically their "scholarships" in many instances result in the preponderance of athletic activities as opposed to "scholarly" activities. In fact, it is their athletic activities that pose the most severe limitations on their opportunities to engage in scholarly pursuits."[51]

In his work on opportunity gaps in US education, Rich Milner argues that the educational system is not structurally designed to create opportunities for some students to develop into the successful students they can become. The work of all these scholars who have studied the educational plight of Black male football and basketball athletes at HWCU challenges us to think more deeply "about how systems, processes, and institutions are overtly and covertly designed to maintain the status quo and sustain depressingly complicated disparities in education," as Milner argues.[52] In the coming chapters, I extend and support this argument by sharing powerful narratives of Black males who identified opportunity gaps they encountered in pursuit of their education as college athletes at HWCU, and offered thoughts on how to address these gaps.

CHAPTER 2

Education Matters Then and Now:
A Case Study of Teammates in a
Big-Time College Football Program

It [the focus group] allows Black males to really talk about what's really going on.

Bobby

We [Black male athletes] need to voice our opinion more . . . athletes in general need to have more to say in things.

Mark

It [the focus group] felt pretty good to get some stuff off your chest and sit back and think about everything that goes on, and just help you get refocused and motivated.

Marcus

I N THIS CHAPTER, I draw inspiration from critical race theory (CRT) to present a case study of Bobby, Marcus, and Mark (these are pseudonyms they chose), three Black male teammates who played key roles in a big-time college football program at a major HWCU. My primary goal is to share these Black males' reflections on pertinent education matters at two distinctive points in their lives: in 2002, when they were nineteen- to twenty-one-year-old college athletes; and in 2018, when they were well into their post-playing lives and careers. I focus on the past, or the *then*, because we need more research that centers around Black male athletes' perspectives on their educational experiences in real time. In regard to the present, or the *now*, reconnecting with these Black male athletes in 2018 was important because it invited them to reflect on their educational experiences and outcomes with the insights gained since they played college sport.

The three Black male athletes I feature in this chapter were initially identified by a Black male academic counselor in athletics who created and directed an academic support and career and life skills program designed particularly to address the culturally relevant interests and needs of Black and other racial minority athletes at this HWCU. Bobby, Marcus, and Mark were specifically chosen because they each played a prominent role on the team, and they demonstrated a strong interest in the topic and a willingness to engage me in critical dialogue about it.

The profiles presented here are based on a background questionnaire that each filled out in 2002; the focus group that I moderated in that year; and individual interviews I conducted with them shortly after the focus group and years later in 2018. I also relied on secondary data sources such as websites; news articles; their social media profiles on LinkedIn, Facebook, and other platforms; and other artifacts of communication. Bobby, Marcus, and Mark were all invited to offer comments and feedback on my initial interpretation of their words and stories, and to provide additional input into their respective narratives that are presented in this case study. This process of welcoming and asking these three Black males to be co-creators of the knowledge about them is a form of member checking that helped me to present accurate and credible information.

This chapter is divided into four major sections. First, I provide the context for this case study, describing particular characteristics of the HWCU and athletic department where these three athletes attended school. Second, I give pertinent information about their general P–12 schooling and family background, academic backgrounds and playing careers in college, and pursuit of professional football playing careers post-graduation. I focus in a bit more detail on what they have been up to since the clock stopped on their college and/or professional playing careers in the last section of this chapter. Third, I draw directly from original research with these three Black males that I have published elsewhere to discuss education matters they deemed to be relevant when they were college athletes.[1] I specifically share their definitions of and thoughts on education, views on the benefits and detriments of college sport participation, understandings of racism, and understandings of institutional integrity in college sport. Finally, I rely on more primary and secondary data sources to address the question, "Where are they now?" More precisely, this section not only discusses the role college sport played in helping these Black males navigate through life after college sport, but perhaps more importantly, where they are in terms of their thinking around matters pertaining to the education of Black male athletes now and in the future.

THE BIG-TIME COLLEGE FOOTBALL PROGRAM

The big-time college football program these Black male athletes played in is situated within an athletic department at one of the largest HWCU in the US. The university has been consistently ranked by *US News & World Report* as a top twenty national public university and as one of "America's Best Colleges." The athletic department is affiliated with one of the major Football Bowl Subdivision (FBS) conferences (FBS programs are the most competitive and high profile in NCAA Division I) and is completely self-supporting, with one of the largest operating budgets among NCAA member institutions.

The tradition-rich football program has won several conference and multiple national championships; produced multiple Heisman Trophy winners; been consistently ranked in the top twenty-five in the Associated Press pools and in Coaches' Polls; and regularly had players drafted into the NFL. Similar to many of its peer institutions in other FBS conferences, football at this HWCU has been the athletic department's economic engine and cash cow. This has allowed the department to contribute financially to the university and support close to a thousand athletes by fully funding about three dozen varsity sport programs. Many of these programs and some of the individual athletes and coaches within them have achieved success on a national and international level.

The athletic department has long been recognized for its excellence. It has been ranked in the top twenty (several top ten finishes more recently) in the standings for the Division I Director's Cup, which has been awarded since 1993 by the National Association of Collegiate Directors of Athletics to the nation's most successful athletics program. The three Black athletes featured in this chapter certainly helped contribute to this athletic department's robust history of athletic excellence and success.

Now let's meet Bobby, Marcus, and Mark!

THE BACKGROUND OF THE THREE BLACK MALE ATHLETES

Bobby

At the time of the original study, Bobby was a nineteen-year-old running back and kick returner on special teams who had recently finished his first year of eligibility as a true freshman who decided not to redshirt during his first year on campus.[2] As a highly touted and heavily recruited football athlete coming into the university, he had attended high school and participated in football, track and field, and baseball in what education scholar Rich Milner has described as an *urban emergent* schooling environment—the population of such cities is typically under one million, but they are still relatively large spaces. Although these cities do not experience the magnitude of challenges that larger *urban intensive* areas like Chicago and Detroit do, they still encounter some of the same scarcity of resources and other challenges, such as qualification of teachers, academic development of students, and school funding.[3] Bobby went to high school in a large Midwestern city. According to the 2000 census, the racial demographics were approximately 68 percent White and 24 percent Black, with the remaining 8 percent consisting of people from other racial backgrounds.

Bobby was a 4.0 student in high school and ranked near the top of his graduating class; he also served as the president of his senior class. Bobby came from a two-parent household, and both his mother and father worked outside the home. Both parents had participated in high school athletics.; his father played football in high school and his mother ran track. Additionally, Bobby has two older brothers who both played college football. One of his brothers also played semi-pro football.

Bobby's decision to attend the university was based in part on its proximity to his home. His family ties were crucial to his decision to stay close to home. Bobby explained,

> I grew up here, so I really wanted my parents to see me play football. Because they'd seen every [high school] game, so it is hard to leave them when, knowing that they can't see some of my [college] games if I went to an institution farther away.

When asked about his athletic aspirations, Bobby expressed a desire to crack the starting lineup as a freshman and eventually win the Heisman

Trophy. Thus, in addition to proximity, Bobby came to this university because "you want to get exposure," which he felt would give him the best shot at making it to the NFL. Although Bobby fell short of his goal of winning the trophy, he was a key contributor, particularly on special teams, throughout his college playing career.

Academically, Bobby excelled, as he had in high school. He graduated from college in four years with a 3.6 GPA. His academic prowess and athletic achievements in both high school and college, made him a *scholar-baller*—a term coined by sport management and higher education scholar C. Keith Harrison to describe middle school, high school, or college athletes who succeed in both the academic and athletic domains.[4] Bobby's academic success serves as an important counter-narrative to the popular Black "dumb jock" myth and other stereotypes like *deficient, disengaged,* and *apathetic* that are typically assigned to Black male athletes.[5] He decided to major in communications because, as he explained, once his playing days were over, "I felt like I wanted to be a sports analyst—you know, cover college and professional football one day. I thought that would be good. I felt like . . . I can talk pretty good and I'm good in front of the camera."

After graduating, Bobby was picked up by an NFL team as an undrafted rookie free agent. But his stint in the NFL was transitory; he ended up injuring his knee before the season and was subsequently cut from the team. This sent him into a "depression mode" and moved him to "let football go altogether" when he realized that his playing career had likely come to an end. In our 2018 interview, Bobby shared with me how having the opportunity to earn his master's degree while working as an intern with the athletic director at his alma mater helped him to some degree move beyond his depression. During that same period, he was able to put his undergraduate degree to use working in front of the camera as a sports analyst for his alma mater and a professional sports team in the area. Bobby credits this experience with helping him discover and eventually find his passion for the acting career path he was on in 2018.

Mark

At the time of the original study, Mark was a twenty-year-old wide receiver who had recently finished his redshirt junior year. He participated in football, basketball, and track and field in high school. The school he attended was in what Rich Milner described as an *urban characteristic* schooling environment. These are sometimes in rural or suburban districts, rather than large or midsize cities, but still might be starting to experience some of the challenges associated with urban intensive and urban emergent environments; for example, increases in English language learners. Mark's high school was located on the outskirts of a large Midwestern urban emergent city. The population of this small suburb was approximately 78 percent White, 11 percent Black, and 10 percent Asian, with the remaining 1 percent from other racial backgrounds. The town had a highly rated public school system. The public high school Mark attended was the only one in the district, and had an enrollment of roughly seventeen hundred students. Mark described it as a racially/ethnically diverse high school in a "nice city," and that the student body "was about 60 percent White and 40 percent Black. It was a pretty good mix."

Mark reported that he was "an average student," with a 2.7 GPA. In his words, "I did enough to get by . . . I could have done a lot more. I probably could have studied more for tests, but there was another thing—like, I was a student-athlete. I was just tired." He grappled with balancing the demands of academics and athletics, and his athletic identity seemed to take precedence over his academic and other identities in high school.

Like Bobby, Mark was raised in a two-parent household. Both his parents were educators. Although his father was a "real fast" athlete in high school, Mark said he and his older brother were the "first ones to excel past high school to play sports" in college. Both brothers played football in big-time college sport programs. When I asked if they played on the same football team in high school, Mark recounted how he came late to the sport. His brother was a football player and he was a basketball player. But then "my senior year, because my coach just kept asking and asking . . . I kind of thought that maybe I would enjoy it and it became secondhand to me." Standing about 6' 5" tall, Mark was able to successfully transfer his athleticism on the basketball court to the position of wide receiver on the football field. He parlayed this into an athletic scholarship to play in the HWCU that all three athletes in this study attended.

When asked why he chose to attend this HWCU, Mark named the scholarship as the main reason. Similar to Bobby, he also gave this university's proximity to his hometown as a reason. His hometown friends' decision to attend school there also played into his decision. Finally, he mentioned the strength of the athletic program as a major influence on his decision. Like Bobby, Mark was attracted to the major television exposure that the football program receives. He insisted, "[It] is just a lot easier chance to go to the NFL from [name of university] than it is from a D3 [Division III]." Mark, like so many other highly talented Black male athletes recruited to HWCU with big-time college sport programs, chose this program over less prestigious Division II, Division III, or HBCU because he saw it as a more promising path toward upward social mobility.

In terms of his athletic aspirations, Mark desired to achieve All-American status at the college level, and then play professional football in the NFL. Although he arguably had the raw talent to develop into an All-American wide receiver in college, his college playing career was plagued by injury, and this likely contributed at least to some degree to his not reaching his full potential. He was also an All-American caliber long jumper in college until a knee injury toward the end of his final football season permanently ended both his college football and track and field careers. But this injury did not deter Mark from pursuing an NFL playing career.

While acknowledging that professional sport can be emotionally taxing, Mark saw it as "one of the easiest ways that you can make money." However, he also acknowledged that a career as a professional athlete is not promised to anyone. He discussed what his post-playing career path might look like, and suggested it would probably involve working within the sport industry in some capacity. Since sport had been such an integral part of his life up to that point, he believed he was "going to be involved with sports for my entire life."

Mark was fortunate enough to rehabilitate his injured knee in time to work out for scouts at the NFL combine. He ended up being drafted in the middle rounds of the NFL draft, but suffered another injury during the preseason before his rookie season, which sidelined him his entire first year. After suffering yet another major knee injury five years into his solid NFL career, Mark decided to retire from the NFL and focus on rehabilitating his knee for quality of life off the field. He put his education degree to use briefly, teaching and coaching high school football. He also worked for a short time as an analyst in the sport media. But similar to Bobby, Mark's career path moved in the direction of acting.

Marcus

At the time of the original study, Marcus was a twenty-one-year-old defensive back who had recently finished his junior year. Like Bobby, Marcus had attended high school and participated in football, basketball, and track and field in an urban emergent schooling environment. However, the environment in which Marcus grew up and attended high school was not nearly as large as the one in which Bobby was raised and schooled. In 2000, the population of this midsized Midwestern city was approximately 74 percent White and 21 percent Black, with the remaining 5 percent from other racial backgrounds. By the 1970s, Bobby's high school was the only one left in the city. This high school had a tradition-rich, highly successful athletic program, particularly in football. According to Marcus, his high school was "predominantly White, but the athletic programs were all Black." He further described it as "a school of about five thousand; you know, two, three thousand White . . . fifteen hundred Black, and then other ethnic backgrounds."

Like Mark, Marcus's athletic identity took precedence over his academic and other identities in high school. Marcus identified himself as a "pretty good student" who "kind of slacked off on my education" once he realized during his sophomore year that "sports would probably help me to get over a little bit." He recounted, "I was sort of concentrating more on my athletics, but at the same time I just did enough . . . just to get by. I graduated with like a 2.6 . . . like a 21 on my ACT and whatever. When I first came in, I was like a 3.0 student." As Marcus's words suggest, once he discovered that his athletic prowess would present him the opportunity to play football at the college level, his academics took a back seat to sports.

Although Marcus was raised in a single-parent home, it was not the single-parent, female-headed household that people stereotypically associate with young Black males. Instead, his uncle was his legal guardian. This particular uncle had played basketball in college and was the only college graduate in his family:

> So I was raised by my uncle . . . since I was about seven years old. He got me started playing sports when I was eight, playing football . . . basketball, baseball, every season. Every sport, that season, I was playing it. So I was a three-season sport guy and [my uncle] just understood the values and coming to be a man at an early age. I was always on my own from basically high school on up with him working . . . nights

and stuff like that. So . . . I had to cook myself dinner, and I learned a little bit and washed clothes and did some stuff, and I had the house to myself, to clean up . . . the yard, cut the grass, and all that different stuff. So I learned how to, you know, be a man . . .

Marcus also talked about his father and his two uncles and how "they are all real close" and each had a hand in helping to raise him. But it was the uncle who raised him and introduced him to sport who allowed him to begin developing into a "man at an early age."

Marcus decided to attend this university primarily for economic reasons. He was also impressed with the "rich tradition" of the football program. In particular, he commented on the nature of his playing position: "This school has been putting defensive backs into the NFL year in and year out, first round." Marcus was able to earn significant playing time very early on in his playing career and was very productive on the field from the end of his first year through his senior year of eligibility. In addition, the school's proximity to his home "played into the mix" when he signed his letter of intent to play football there.

Marcus was talented and accomplished enough to enter the NFL draft after his junior year, but he decided to come back for his final year of eligibility in pursuit of a national championship. When asked about his athletic aspirations, Marcus first discussed his goals at the college level: "My goal is to win a national championship for this university . . . I've been winning championships since I was eight on every level I played. So Pee Wee to middle school to high school . . . And my goal is to do that here. So that's why I came back to this university for my last year." After completing his senior year, Marcus planned to "reach the NFL and be the best wherever in my position and win championships." He wanted to "dominate the sport" at every possible level.

To prepare for life after his professional playing career, Marcus majored in communications. He talked about the number of former athletes who have been able to establish themselves as television commentators. In light of this fact, Marcus thought "Maybe after I get done playing, I can go ahead and do that because I will be very familiar with playing and knowing what goes on, on and off the field, and just being able to talk about it."

After his senior year, Marcus was drafted in the early rounds of the NFL draft. He had some success as an NFL defensive back for multiple teams; but he battled injuries throughout his professional career, and this was likely a factor in it lasting only six seasons. Shortly after being cut from the last team he played for, he began a career in corporate America, in sales. He was also inducted into the hall of fame for his college alma mater a few years after his NFL career ended.

EDUCATION MATTERS THEN

I begin this section by sharing what the concept of education meant to Bobby, Marcus, and Mark during their college playing days. I then illuminate some of the psychosocial benefits and detriments these Black males identified as germane to their college sport participation. This contributes to the important question and conversation on education as a legitimation of college sport that I introduced in chapter 1. Given the history and legacy of racism in US society and its educational system, this conversation is significant. My related discussion with them about matters of institutional integrity in college sport is important for two reasons. First, it revealed what these Black male athletes believed to be particular ethical issues and unjust policies and practices that college sport leaders should address to better serve the interests and needs of athletes. Second, it invited these Black male athletes to voice their thoughts and offer ideas and suggestions for change.

Defining Education

Part of my discussion was to ask each athlete to share with me what the concept of education meant to him. This allowed me to better understand and properly articulate pertinent education matters that were raised during the 2002 study. On the concept of education, Bobby reflected:

> Education is . . . pretty much everything that has to do with your own life. A lot of people think education is just . . . you come to college and get your degree, and "I got education now, because I got my degree" . . . I mean, that's part of it, but that's not the big picture . . . Education, when you go to college, is about learning about yourself, about finding new things out that you didn't know about yourself and other people.

Similar to the description of education that I gave in the introduction, Bobby believed education for Black male athletes extended beyond simply earning a college degree. He suggested it involved acquiring a greater knowledge of your history and who you are, and more knowledge about people who are different from yourself.

Marcus offered similar and even more profound ideas on the concept of education. In sharing his insights, he seemed to allude to the great scholar W. E. B. DuBois's notion of *double consciousness* in suggesting that Black people must have a certain type of knowledge to successfully navigate their way through society.[6]

> To me, education is just being able to grasp knowledge and know exactly what's going on around you in each environment . . . because you can't be in a ghetto and communicate with them and then go over here to White society and communicate with them, you know, unless you have some sense of education.

This description implies that education for Black people involves having the opportunity not only to understand the different social contexts they might find themselves in, but also to effectively communicate with people across these contexts. In other words, Black male athletes' education is tied to their ability to *code-switch*—that is, to function in the communities they might have grown up in or come from, as well as within White mainstream social institutions and settings such as HWCU.

In exploring the notion of education, Marcus also shed light on how the current educational system has been more conducive to the history, traditions, and interests of White people, not Black people:

> They've taught us the language and taught us, you know, all that educational and whatever . . . so, they kind of have a feel more genetically as far as just absorbing the educational. It took a while for, you know, Blacks to actually try to accept and understand the things that were being taught to them.

In seeking clarification of this statement, I asked Marcus, "Are you suggesting that we as Black people have struggled to learn White people's ways of knowing, their system of education?" Marcus responded, "Right! Their education was initially taught to us . . . they eventually made us learn it. We were slaves and then we probably got our freedom." With these words, Marcus was suggesting that even after the abolition of chattel slavery, Black people were still forced to learn what White people wanted to teach them. Throughout this dialogue, Marcus implied that White athletes have an advantage over Black athletes in terms of education because they are essentially learning about themselves in the curriculum and in White educational spaces, while Blacks are not exposed to educational curriculum and experiences that are culturally relevant to them.

Marcus's understanding of education as a historically Eurocentric, White enterprise, seemed to suggest that education for Blacks involves having an awareness of one's environment, a certain level of independence, and the ability to control things going on in life:

> But as far as education, it is just being able to have a maturity and understand exactly what's going on around you. I'm saying it is like being able to control your own life . . . you have to be able to make your own ideas, your own points, and your own thoughts and go through your own actions.

In his view, education is a developmental process that grows and empowers Black people to become independent, self-sufficient human beings.

In reflecting on education and the role it plays in his growth and development as a Black male, Mark expressed ideas similar to those of his teammates. When asked what education meant to him, he answered,

> Higher learning—just, you know, learning about your life . . . not just being in the class and not just being book smart, but learning about what goes on in real life. How you have got to deal with it. How you don't have nobody like your parents to be there for you. You are on your own . . . being independent is definitely a main part of education.

Both Mark and Marcus stressed how education involves learning to become self-sufficient and independent, and how to deal effectively with the vicissitudes of life.

Benefits and Detriments of College Sport Participation

Although Bobby, Mark, and Marcus acknowledged that they derived certain benefits while playing college sport, they, like sport scholars Ellen Staurowsky and Allen Sack, viewed the term *student-athlete* as an inappropriate label and inaccurate description of who they were.[7] Instead, they argued that terms such as *scholarship athlete* and *athlete-student* (Marcus's term) were more accurate descriptors of their realities as athletes in this big-time college football program. Marcus summed it up well:

> [W]e are here to play a sport, but we also go to school; so they try to collaborate those two and try to say "student-athlete"; we want to be students first, but more, we're athletes first because time's so demanding.

Marcus was aware that the inordinate amount of time college athletes were expected to devote to football-related activities limited their opportunities to pursue other educational experiences outside of football (I will discuss this in more detail below). In his book *Unpaid Professionals*, economist Andrew Zimbalist argued that the "fine line" that exists between the psychosocial benefits and detriments of college sport participation and the hyper-commercialized sports of football and basketball threatens to make the balance between these benefits and detriments a negative one.[8]

Psychosocial Benefits. Despite the fact that the detriments of college sport participation might outweigh the benefits—a fact recognized by Zimbalist and others, as well as by Bobby, Mark, and Marcus—these Black male athletes did acknowledge that their participation in college football had many positive benefits. For one, they viewed college sport participation as great preparation for some of the challenges they would face in life beyond sport. In particular, Bobby had a lot to say about the parallels between life and college football participation, and how the latter helps prepare athletes for the former:

> [A]s a human being, you have to learn about life, you have to just learn about the ups and downs that you're gonna go through, and that's what pretty much being a student-athlete is about too. You know, it's about preparation. If you're prepared . . . you're gonna do good in life, just like you will on a test or on the football field. So I think, you know, it goes hand in hand.

He further stated,

> You're not always gonna win, of course, and you're always gonna have ups and downs in your sport. Where you might have a great game one game and then the next game you come back and you're just terrible.

And you just gotta live with that defeat in you—just grow and get better. And that's pretty much the same thing you have to do in life, because everything's not gonna go your way.

Finally, Bobby alluded to how the intellect and physical prowess required to be successful on the football field is transferable and applicable to life:

Football . . . it causes a lot of thinking. You have to think and react very quickly. So . . . it helps you in life, I think, because . . . you have to think things through about everything pretty much in life, and that's how you have to think in football. You know, somebody who is right here and somebody is right there so . . . if they do this, you gotta do that, and that's how it is in life, pretty much. You know that something, if this goes wrong, then you got this to fall back on, pretty much so. It is just about being prepared.

Mark echoed these sentiments when he suggested that being a college athlete helped him learn the "techniques to survive on the field and off the field." Essentially, Bobby and his teammates believed their participation in the game of college football helped prepare them for the game of life.

Another benefit these Black male athletes reaped from their participation in college sport was the opportunities they had to experience things they might otherwise have not been afforded if they did not play. For example, as members of this high-profile college football program, Marcus and his teammates were granted opportunities to travel and interact with and learn from people from different places and backgrounds. As Marcus put it,

With this whole sport thing, I got to see a lot that I wouldn't see in the world. You know, I traveled, and just seen different parts of the world. Where with sports that kind of connection to other things around the country . . . you might just travel out here and see like different people, how different people live, different ethnic groups or whatever, and see how different cultures live.

Psychosocial Detriments. In the initial focus group and follow-up individual interviews, Bobby, Mark, and Marcus also discussed the struggle associated with balancing the student and athlete roles in this big-time college football program. As mentioned above, all three realized that the time demands of football participation rendered the *student-athlete* label inaccurate. In comparing their experiences with those of students at the university who did not play NCAA Division I football or other varsity sports, they had some interesting perspectives. During our individual interview, Mark described what the term meant to him:

> I just think about student-athletes going through a lot of struggle like school-wise, academic-wise, and sport-wise . . . they have to overcome and become a different class . . . I think student-athletes in some aspects are—I don't know about smarter, but like, have it a lot more together than some regular college students.

He backed this statement up by arguing that college athletes have a lot more on their plate than their peers who are just "regular college students":

> [Y]ou got to study; you got practice; you are tired and the average college student is, you know, two classes a day and maybe has a job. But . . . I don't know, depends on what time their classes are, but if they have classes in the morning, then they are done for the rest of the day. They have time to do their homework. Their body is not tired.

This quote highlights not only the time demands and the physical toll playing college football placed on these Black male college athletes, but also how these burdens are not placed on their non-athlete peers. This is certainly something I have observed and been told by Division I athletes at the HWCU with which I have been affiliated as a student and faculty member for nearly three decades.

Mark's teammates also offered commentary on the differences between their non-athlete peers and themselves. Marcus contended,

> [T]hey don't put in the time that we put in. I'll say that if most student-athletes had a scholarship and were just a student, they would have a 3.0 and 4.0, because they know what it takes . . . from all that time they do with athletics . . . If we took maybe half the time for athletics and put that more into the school work then the graduation rate would be higher.

Bobby shared similar sentiments in his individual interview with me:

> I feel like a lot of student-athletes, even if we didn't play sports . . .
> we could be better than, I think, anybody because sports are so time
> demanding. So mentally . . . just taking you out. Where you know,
> regular students—all they have to worry about is books and learning
> what they need to learn. But we have all this time on our sport, and
> then we have to come back to education, to learn.

Given these athletes' references to the inordinate amount of time they
were expected to devote to football often at the expense of other educational activities outside football, I wanted them to share with me what
their daily schedule looks like. Marcus described a typical day during the
football season:

> [Y]ou wake up and it's already like 7:00, so eight hours of that day are
> already gone . . . Then say that you got class from 9 to 1, you know . . .
> half of the day is already gone. So then you put six hours straight to
> football—six to seven hours straight to football . . . they want you to
> lift and run to get better; you want to watch film and study and learn
> the plays cause you got to go out there and practice it . . .

Marcus further acknowledged that in season it is harder to pursue educational opportunities outside of football "because you want to concentrate
on your athletics and be successful in that, so you put more time into that,
and that kind of hurts your school a little bit because you want to push
athletics."

This rigorous schedule made it difficult for these Black male athletes to
do anything not related to football. In some cases, these and other athletes
are simply out of gas, and this negatively affects their ability to function or
do some of the most basic things that perhaps non-athlete students take for
granted, such as staying awake in class. Marcus explained that the demands
football places on them is why some athletes are "in class knocked out"—
because they are tired. According to Mark, "You are tired; you ain't going
to do no homework." He further discussed how college athletes come in
at night after a long day "and you don't feel like doing anything. You don't
feel like eating, you are so tired."

Mark shed important light on the tough predicament he and his teammates are placed in when they are asked to choose between investing time
in football activities or academics and other areas of development during
the season. In particular, he mentioned the NCAA's "twenty-hour rule,"
which states that programs are only supposed to conduct practices and
football-related activities with their athletes for a maximum of twenty
hours per week and no more than four hours per day during the season.
According to Mark, this rule was never really taken seriously or enforced
by the coaches:

> They got that twenty-hour rule, and I remember so-and-so coach was,
> like, we got to sign a thing saying that we did twenty hours, but every-
> body was laughing . . . Even though we were breaking the rule, we
> were not going to say anything because we would not get on the field.

As is the case at many other major Division I programs, it was a common
practice for the coaching staff to violate the NCAA's twenty-hour rule, and
there was an unspoken law that if these athletes desired to get on the field
and earn playing time, they would have to ignore the rule. Bobby felt that
athletes like himself were constantly being put in compromising positions
where they had to make a choice between devoting their time to football
or other educational experiences. These Black male athletes' revelations are
consistent with other research (for example, Kenneth Shropshire and Colin
Williams Jr.'s, *The Miseducation of the Student Athlete*[9]) that has revealed
Black college athletes often spend more sport-related hours per week in
season than academic time.

While acknowledging that the time demands placed on college athletes
are not as great during the off-season (technically, from January to August),
Marcus, Bobby, and Mark all agreed that, given the hyper-competitive
nature of big-time college football, the time commitment is often just as
intense. Between spring football and various football meetings and other
so-called "voluntary" workouts, their schedules remained packed. In fact,
this schedule presented challenges for me when trying to set up individual
interviews after the initial focus group. These Black male athletes were
right at the beginning of spring football, which is a series of fourteen to
fifteen practice sessions over a roughly three-week period that culminates

in an intrasquad scrimmage. I had a particularly difficult time catching up with Marcus; we eventually met on the first official day of spring football. When Marcus finally arrived (late) for the interview, he had just come from morning football meetings. He apologized and shared with me that he had been up and at it since before 7 a.m., and it was evident throughout the interview that he was not well rested.

Matters of Racism

CRT insists that we acknowledge the experiential knowledge of people of color and other marginalized groups in analyzing matters of law and broader society. In the focus group and individual interviews, Bobby, Marcus, and Mark were invited to reveal and share their perspectives on matters of racism they might have experienced themselves or observed playing college sport at HWCU. I began the focus group by asking them to reflect on the role of sport in US society, and how it has changed historically. This question triggered a conversation about racism in US sport, particularly college sport. Based on this initial dialogue, I used the individual interviews with these Black males to further explore their thinking about this issue.

Two basic themes emerged: access discrimination and treatment discrimination.[10] *Access discrimination* involves behaviors by those in power or some decision-making capacity that unjustly prevent members of certain social groups from obtaining a job, position, or opportunity in a particular organization or profession. The Black athletes in this case study asserted that Blacks are denied consistent access to the major leadership and decision-making positions both on the playing field (in particular, the quarterback role) and off the playing field (athletic directors, team owners, and the like) in college and professional sport. *Treatment discrimination*, on the other hand, typically occurs after members of that social group are in a particular organization or position, at which point they might be exposed to negative behaviors by people who hold different and even similar positions, be denied access to fewer growth and development opportunities within and outside the organization or position, or have differential access to resources. Bobby, Marcus, and Mark each provided examples of how Black males in their athletic department and football program seemed to be treated differently than their White counterparts, and unfairly labeled and stereotyped. The narratives below illustrate these matters and their potential effect on the education of Black male college athletes.

Access Discrimination. All three athletes in this study were very open about their concerns with what they perceived to be a lack of access Black male athletes had to important leadership positions and opportunities both on and off the field. They suggested that certain playing positions are basically off limits to Black athletes. Specifically, the issue of Black athletes being denied access to the quarterback position at these HWCU continually emerged throughout the focus group and individual interviews. While acknowledging that Black athletes have achieved some measure of success as quarterbacks at the professional level, Bobby, Mark and Marcus all suggested that there is plenty of room for improvement at the college level. Marcus commented on this issue during the focus group:

> [H]ere at [university] . . . we ain't got no Black quarterback . . . So you look at different NFL teams that got the McNabbs; they got the Steve McNairs . . . I mean, certain universities still won't have like a Black athlete at quarterback . . . it's just that their so-called tradition where they're trying to uphold.

As a Black male who was conscious of his status as a racialized being, Marcus further asserted in his individual interview that

> racism exists in sports because—I mean, we talked about it in the group, about the Black quarterback, and then how they always want a White quarterback to lead. You have to be an exceptional Black athlete to be a quarterback.

As these athletes acknowledged, Black quarterbacks at these HWCU were becoming more prevalent in the 1990s into the early 2000s when these interviews took place.[11] However, it was Marcus's belief that there was still great resistance to having Black athletes in this most important leadership position on the football field.

I was curious to learn more from Marcus and his peers why HWCU football programs have historically been reluctant to turn over the leadership reins to Black athletes on the field and regularly put them in the quarterback position. Mark quickly offered his viewpoint during the focus group:

> [F]irst of all, it's tradition . . . they're going to think that . . . a Black quarterback's not capable of . . . thinking and remembering the plays and remembering all of that stuff. But then I think they're scared of what we can do . . . if we take over the game, then we're going to dominate [that quarterback position].

Mark's teammates emphatically agreed with this point, chiming in with "Right!" and "Yep!" On occasion, they even finished each other's points or sentences. A case in point is when Mark was further discussing this idea of the White establishment seeing Black athletes as threatening to take over and dominate the college game as leaders both on and off the field:

> [Y]ou got a lot more White coaches than Black coaches, and they see it as we're athletes . . . Black players as athletes—but they can't see us in the main position role . . . They enjoy us being around but they still don't want us to be . . .

At this point, Marcus jumped in and said, "The dominant, the leader."

Bobby, Marcus, and Mark also expressed particular concerns with what they perceived to be a limited opportunity structure for Blacks beyond the playing field. They believed Black athletes have to totally dominate on the field just to have a chance to secure opportunities for leadership positions off the field. As Bobby stated,

> The Black person has to be that much better than the White person, for the Black person to get it.

Mark agreed:

> We have to excel more. To become a head coach . . . you got to excel on the field and then you get respect.

Mark further illuminated his point during his individual interview. In discussing how the majority of senior-level leaders and administrators who make the final hiring decisions are White, he suggested that if Black applicants for these leadership positions in college sport don't have the social network ties that many of their White counterparts do, they must perform extraordinary feats on the playing field to even be seriously considered:

> [T]he only way that you can get that job is if you win two Heisman Trophies or something outstanding where everybody already loves you. It is like, "Oh, since we love them, we are going to get them." But if you are just somebody applying for a job, and they see ethnic background . . . and they get an interview, they are going to be like, "Oh, what did you do?"

These narratives indicate that Marcus, Bobby, and Mark were keenly aware of the adverse impact institutional racism at HWCU had on opportunities for Black male athletes like them to pursue careers in leadership positions in the very institutions their labor helped build.

Treatment Discrimination. Marcus, Bobby, and Mark all expressed frustration with how Black male athletes were negatively treated by people within the athletic department and broader campus environment. Bobby was particularly troubled by the disparities he observed regarding the scheduling of classes for athletes in the athletic department. According to Bobby, Black athletes have too often been scheduled for

> classes they really don't need, and that's why they are here forever, because they are taking all the classes they don't need, where the White guy, he's just, you know, "All classes you need . . . " or even if he [White guy] doesn't know, they might—I think they might give him a little advantage. They might tell him, "Well, you need this," where the Black person, they just, you know, "We just want you to play football pretty much."

Bobby further specified,

> Sometimes I feel like the academic counselors, . . . I don't know if they don't think that Black people are just as smart as the White people are, because you know, when it comes to the Black people . . . they just want to get us by, by giving us any old class . . . Where [with] the

White person, they are, like, "Well, you need to take this, this, and this."
Where with the Black person, they are, like, "Well, we'll give you this"
. . . "You just take this" . . . Sometimes it's like that."

When I asked Bobby how he dealt with this particular matter, he
exclaimed, "I don't let them pick my schedule . . . I know what classes I
need to take . . . I'm not giving them a choice to try to conform me!" His
response is a powerful example of what scholar Joseph Cooper meant by
strategic responsiveness to interest convergence.[12] That is, Bobby had the
wherewithal to recognize the exploitative nature of this situation and take
appropriate counteractions to prevent it from adversely affecting his educational experiences.

Mark also discussed differential treatment of Black male athletes he
had observed during his time on campus. When I asked him about racism in college sport during our individual interview, he discussed several
examples of situations where Black male athletes were racially stereotyped
and unfairly treated in comparison to their White male counterparts. He
shared how faculty at the university treated Black male athletes: "You got
teachers here that I think judge right away. That 'This person, okay, he is
tall, but he is Black and he is going to be lazy and he is not going to make
a good effort.'"

Bobby's insights supported Mark's experiences and observations:

[I]n the classroom, I know a lot of people—well I mean, sometimes it is
just athletes, but sometimes it is just, its Black athletes that . . . teachers
don't like or teachers think they're gonna cause a problem in their class.

Bobby specifically stressed how these faculty and others in the campus
community tend to stereotype Black male athletes as troublemakers or
"dumb jocks," especially if they are dressed in "baggy clothes" or their
"pants are sagging." The research literature supports these sentiments, and
subsequent field-based, qualitative studies with Black male college athletes
corroborate these narratives. For example, one of the former Black male
college athletes in sociologist Krystal Beamon's study on racism and stereotyping on HWCU campuses discussed how his large size and his "real
black" complexion made him stand out in the classroom setting, and how

that disadvantaged him because professors assumed he "must be dumb."[13] Indeed, the Black "dumb jock" myth was prevalent when I interviewed the Black male athletes for this study, and it continues to be alive and well on HWCU campuses to this day.

In our individual interview, Mark offered additional insight into differences between how Black male athletes are perceived and treated in comparison to their White male peers. When asked to elaborate on the manifestation of racism in college sport, Mark discussed a situation where one of his former teammates, who is Black, was seemingly always singled out for drug testing:

> [M]y friend played football here two years ago, and he, I guess you could say, he is a dark guy . . . He is real dark, but he somehow, every-time . . . he doesn't do drugs or anything, but every drug test he will be picked . . .

At this point, I asked, "Isn't drug testing supposed to be random?" Mark responded:

> [I]t is random, but every single time, he would be picked somehow. It is supposed to be totally random . . . I know plenty of White boys on the team that do drugs but never get checked. Because they think, and if I looked at the person, the White boy, I would be like, "He doesn't do drugs," but when I seen [sic] it, I was like, "Dang!"

Mark's narrative suggests there was a double standard applied to Black male athletes during his time at the HWCU.

This situation was one of multiple examples where Mark believed his White teammates were afforded certain privileges that Black athletes were typically not granted. The CRT tenet of Whiteness as a property interest speaks to these examples of White male athletes being granted unearned and undeserved privileges and opportunities simply because they are White. Another example Mark shared was a time where the starting quarterback of the team, a White male, was arrested and charged with driving under the influence of alcohol, but was later reinstated to the team. According to Mark,

When they recruited the person, he was a defensive back but he was turned . . . into a quarterback. But if it was a Black athlete, you know, right when things went bad they'd move him back . . . to a DB.

Mark further elaborated, "That person who played quarterback, he made more mistakes off the field and still got shots," He insisted that "if it was a Black athlete," that person would not have gotten those same second and third chances. It was Mark's perception that Black male athletes were held to much higher standards and expectations than their White counterparts and were punished more severely when they made mistakes or errors in judgement.

Matters of Institutional Integrity

Given the issues and challenges that Marcus, Bobby, and Mark identified, I was interested in learning more from them about matters that impacted their educational experiences and outcomes as well as any recommendations they had to address the seeming lack of institutional integrity at this and other HWCU where Black male athletes populate the major revenue-producing football and basketball programs. In discussing the need to nurture the intellectual and academic development of Black college athletes, higher education educator Bobby Daniels described *institutional integrity* as an "institution's degree of consistency between their rhetoric and their behavior relative to stated commitments to the development of all students' intellectual and social development, including student-athletes."[14] The NCAA and its member institutions have long used rhetoric around making the educational experiences of college athletes "paramount." Similar to its peer institutions, the mission statement of the athletic department where Marcus, Bobby, and Mark played football expressed its commitment to providing athletes with educational opportunities for personal growth and the ability to engage with a diverse and changing society. In other words, it pledged to create a combination of favorable circumstances that prioritized the education of college athletes over everything else. But the narratives offered below suggest that opportunity gaps existed; institutional structures, policies, and practices at the NCAA level and in this athletic department and at this HWCU made circumstances less favorable than they could and should have been for these Black male athletes to ma. their educational experiences and outcomes.

In regard to the NCAA and this HWCU and its athletic department, Marcus, Bobby, and Mark focused on matters related to the lack of diversity in the leadership structures, lack of financial support for athletes, and the lack of opportunities for athlete empowerment. First, they emphasized the need for the inclusion of more Black administrators, coaches, and academic support personnel and other leaders in these institutions. Second, they lamented the financial hardships that Black athletes often experience and the blatant hypocrisy in the NCAA policies on athlete compensation. And finally, they stressed their appreciation for the opportunity their participation in this study afforded them to "get some stuff off your chest" (Marcus), and mentioned the importance of providing safe havens and platforms for Black athletes to lift their voices and be heard.

Black Role Models in Leadership. During the early stages of the focus group interview and throughout some of the individual interviews, the participants metaphorically referred to Black male athletes in big-time college sport at HWCU as "glorified slaves" and "high-class slaves" (Marcus). The implication was that although they are in the spotlight and are given some celebrity treatment and perks, they are being exploited for their athletic prowess to the detriment of other critical areas of their overall education and development. This discussion encouraged me to ask these athletes for recommendations on how to address this challenge. Mark responded, "We need to get more Black people in higher positions because . . . Black athletes will be able to relate and adjust better to college." Mark's observations correspond with findings from Ketra Armstrong and Michael Jennings's study with Black male football players who "experienced cultural misplacement" because of the lack of racial representation in their Division I HWCU athletic department.[15]

Toward the end of the focus group interview, I asked Bobby, Mark, and Marcus to offer closing comments. One by one, they expressed thoughts and feelings about the state of the Black male in sport in general and in college sport in particular. All of them acknowledged Black males' predominance in sport as athletes on the fields and courts of play but noted the lack of opportunities for them to serve as managers and leaders in these contexts. Mark opined that while it was "good" that Black males have been afforded opportunities to demonstrate their dominance as athletes, Black males like him also need opportunities to be the boss or "the person that somebody's working for instead of I'm working for them." Bobby agreed with Mark's points and suggested that opportunities for Black people to lead in sport and society have "increased from back when . . . but we're not at the top" as owners, university presidents, athletic directors, head coaches, and other positions of power. Although this pattern of thinking that Blacks should be more highly visible in the dominant leadership positions off the field continuously emerged throughout my conversations with these Black males, Marcus did caution his teammates about suggesting that Blacks should be dominating all facets of sport, because we live in a racially and ethnically diverse world and it is not realistic to expect for "everything to be 100 percent Black."

Marcus, Bobby, and Mark agreed on the need for more Black people in upper-level leadership positions, but they were particularly interested in seeing more Black people in other key support positions and roles in the athletic department and on the HWCU campuses. In a conversation I had with Bobby about whether or not these HWCU were doing enough to address the needs of Black athletes, he suggested, "I think they can always do more just as far as . . . getting more Black academic advisers in here." Bobby and his teammates wanted more academic support staff like the Black male academic adviser who initially connected me with them. They also wanted "more color on the university" (Bobby) more generally, including Black faculty, who could better relate to Black athletes and help them deal with some of the sociocultural issues they face in the exploitive environment of these HWCU. This important matter has been discussed in the literature by Eddie Comeaux and his colleagues.[16]

Financial Support. The controversial issue of financial support and athlete compensation has become more pronounced in the decades since the integration of Black male athletes into football and basketball programs at HWCU. Proponents of the academic capitalist model of college sport governance have argued that the athletic scholarship is sufficient financial support for college athletes, whereas proponents of the athlete rights model for college sport reform have insisted it is not enough, especially given the revenue the NCAA and its member institutions amass from the labor of these athletes. This debate was not lost on Marcus, Bobby, and Mark. During our focus group discussion, they raised this issue and how the NCAA and HWCU need to provide greater financial support for college athletes, particularly for Black athletes, who, in many cases, come to these HWCU from low socioeconomic backgrounds. Marcus was especially outspoken on this matter:

> I mean, it's a money issue . . . we are minorities; we don't come from backgrounds where we can have money to come back on, because a lot of times we are out here really struggling . . . You might get, have one, one-and-a-half meals a day, and still have to get up the next day and go to football practice or go to class; and a lot of people just don't have the money or the financial backing . . . to help move you forward . . .

Mark interposed, "You can't get a job," suggesting that even though the NCAA has implemented rules that allow athletes to work and earn some money throughout the year, the time demands associated with big-time college sport participation makes it extremely difficult to get a job outside the two full-time jobs of being a college athlete and registered student. Then Marcus continued:

> That's why some people are stuck, not knowing their purpose because they don't have enough backing to help them move forward . . . just to be able to enjoy all of the perks of college. If you don't have the finances to be able to enjoy all these different things and see all these different things then, how can you enjoy it? You can't . . .

Marcus, Mark, and Bobby discussed how athletic scholarships and Pell grants "only go so far" (Bobby) in addressing the financial struggles of college athletes. Their general sentiment was that a lack of financial support too often inhibits Black athletes' ability to fully live and enjoy the college experience.

Given these perspectives on the financial hardships Black athletes face in big-time college sport, I was interested in their perceptions of what can be done to address this matter. During our focus group discussion about the large amount of revenue Black male athletes help generate for the athletic department but the inequitable distribution of financial resources that come back to them, they said in unison, "They need to give us more money." They felt that everyone except the athletes seemed to be getting an equitable piece of the financial pie. They were especially troubled by the fact that their coaches could receive special perks and monetary rewards, but they could not. As Marcus exclaimed, "They are getting all this stuff; they are driving cars . . . my question is, how can the coach get a dealer tag car for six months, but I can't?" Bobby demanded, "Who is watching us? The fans are watching us; they ain't watching coaches." And Marcus put an exclamation point on this part of the discussion:

> The NCAA ain't watching the coach . . . The NCAA is watching the players to make sure we ain't out there taking extra benefits . . . to us, it ain't no extra benefits, you know what I'm saying? We are struggling! We need this!

These sentiments suggest that because athletes, not their coaches, are the primary labor force of big-time college sport, the NCAA should address these disparities in financial compensation. Similar to previous research with college athletes on amateurism and athlete compensation dating back to the 1980s, Marcus, Bobby, and Mark all questioned the NCAA's archaic rules on athlete compensation, and believed their policies on athlete compensation were unjust and needed to be reformed.[17]

Platform to Voice Concerns. One of the more powerful recommendations to come out of my conversations with Marcus, Bobby, and Mark was that they desired more opportunities to engage in critical conversations such as the one we had in this particular study. Toward the end of the focus group and individual interviews, I asked each of them to share their thoughts about the study. Marcus reflected on how he enjoyed the focus group experience, sharing with his teammates about their individual and collective experiences. He appreciated the opportunity to "sit back and think about everything that goes on" because it was helping him to "get refocused and motivated." Bobby and Mark also spoke about the value of the focus group and individual interview experiences:

> I think this is good because it allows Black males to really talk about what's really going on. And a lot of people, they don't really know. You know, they don't really know what a Black male student-athlete goes

through. You know, in society as far as academically, and you know mentally and on the football field and off. So, I think it is a good thing. (Bobby)

We need to voice our opinion more. We need to be able—athletes in general need to have more to say in things. Not just, not like robots. We are not people that should just be told to do whatever. We are doing this and we don't have any say because we don't have any money. That is a shame. (Mark)

In line with the critical race research tradition, these Black males athletes were able to speak their minds and at the same time critically reflect on their educational experiences and needs. This research study is but one example of the kinds of platforms Black male athletes should be given to voice their concerns and speak truth to power. Once I assured them that confidentiality would be maintained, they were willing to offer candid thoughts on various matters that impacted their education.

WHERE ARE THEY NOW?

In this section, I provide an update on what Bobby, Mark, and Marcus were up to at the time of my writing, their reflections on how college sport prepared them for their careers and life's work, and general thoughts on Black male athletes' education matters going forward.

Bobby

In 2018, Bobby had a wife and children and had begun to establish himself as an actor in Los Angeles. Since booking his first small role on a major network, he has slowly but surely secured more roles and opportunities in the profession. Bobby reflected on how his participation in major college football has helped prepare him for the here and now, "being in the business I'm in now, where 90 percent of the opportunities that I have to audition are *no's*." He told me how playing college football at that high-profile level helped him develop the discipline, resilience, and in particular, the strong work ethic that is needed to stay the course and continue to navigate the many obstacles before him as he pursues an acting career:

I think that is something that is really helping me today than anything else—understanding what work ethic looks like, understanding what hard work looks like and how that transcends from average hard work to extra effort gets you here, and to the next-level kind of thing. So I would say that those things have helped me to where I am now.

As he reflected back on some of the topics and themes from our 2002 conversations, he also recalled how some of the academic counselors in athletics only seemed interested in scheduling Black athletes for classes they thought would be easy to get an A in, not necessarily classes they needed or could truly benefit from taking. He used the example of foreign-language classes, and shared how although he did not take the class that these counselors typically tried to cluster Black athletes into, he ended up taking a different class simply "to get my foreign language requirement done in a year." In hindsight, he wishes that he would have had the proper guidance or foresight to study a foreign language that he could actually use for practical purposes and to directly benefit him in his acting career. He observed, "Now I live in Los Angeles, where, if I spoke Spanish, it would help me out tremendously. And now I have to learn Spanish."

When asked to compare education matters that impacted Black male college athletes a when he was playing with those impacting Black male college athletes now, Bobby shared that he believes "colleges are actively trying to help athletes a little bit more now." He described how he has been following the recruitment process of his young nephew, who was being recruited by several major football programs at HWCU. His observation has been these programs are "focusing on academics almost just as much as the football aspect of it." Bobby did acknowledge that his teammates and he had great access to academic support when he played, "but the view was still, like, 'You're here to play football.'" And although that view still holds true across many of these big-time college football programs in the here and now, Bobby's perception was that "the mind-set a little bit has changed" to one of focusing on better preparing these college athletes for life after football because "it's been brought up a little bit more . . . and I feel like colleges feel they have to do something about it." Bobby is unsure how much effort these HWCU are putting into helping prepare college athletes for life after sport, but he does believe it has now become much more of a conversation on these campuses and in various other contexts.

To end our 2018 conversation, I asked Bobby for his concluding thoughts on the intersection of race, sport, and education and things I should consider as I was finishing up the project. Bobby offered two major points. First, he stressed how these HWCU should never lose sight of the fact that they are often dealing with eighteen- to twenty-two-year-old young Black males who have been socialized to focus solely or primarily on participation in sport, and therefore "there needs to be multiple mentors that surround them to the point of not just supporting their football dreams, but also encouraging their educational dreams." Bobby's suggestion is in alignment with sport management scholars Darren Kelly and Marlene Dixon's framework for how constellation mentoring can be used by HWCU as a valuable tool for addressing the multiple and diverse needs of Black male athletes as they transition into college sport at HWCU in particular.[18]

Second, Bobby revisited our 2002 conversation about athlete compensation and financial support for Black male college athletes. He reflected on his time as an intern with the athletic director at his alma mater and seeing firsthand "how much money they're making just off of one game" that these Black male athletes play in on any given Saturday, or in some cases, other days of the week. Bobby pushed back against the common argument that college athletes are getting a fair deal because tuition, housing, books, and fees are being paid for via the athletic scholarship. While acknowledging the value of such scholarships, Bobby was not buying the argument that athletic scholarships are sufficient compensation for college athletes. He reiterated some of the points he and his teammates made in 2002 about how "a hundred thousand fans are not coming to see" the head football coaches who are making millions of dollars off the backs of Black male football and basketball athletes. Bobby called out the NCAA's inequitable polices on athlete compensation, and the negative impact they often have on Black athletes from low socioeconomic backgrounds in particular. He noted how "something's not right" when the NCAA, its member institutions, and other entities in the college sport enterprise turn college athletes into commodities to be bought and sold—not only their bodies but their jerseys, their likenesses, and other memorabilia—and then think they are being fair when they pay for them to come to college and offer them an inadequate education. This, according to Bobby, is "something we need to focus on" going forward.

Mark

Similar to Bobby, with whom he sometimes meets to collaborate with and bounce ideas off of, Mark pursued an acting career—"something that I always wanted to do"—after playing sport. When we reconnected, Mark shared with me how not having a wife and children and the smart way in which he saved and invested the money from his NFL playing career helped ease his transition out of professional football and allowed him to eventually immerse himself in Los Angeles. Mark made it clear that while being a former professional athlete might "maybe get you in the door," he has had to humble himself and grind it out to break into the acting profession. Mark has done several readings for roles, worked in internships at top production companies, performed in national commercials, hosted a few shows, and taken the approach of "just progressively building your resume and just working for the next thing."

In reflecting on how his participation in big-time college football has prepared him for a career in the acting business, Mark found it to be "mindboggling" just "how much this industry or this life in general runs so parallel to all my sport, everything I've played, everything that you've done, and the lessons that you learn doing a sport." He discussed the resiliency, mental toughness, overcoming obstacles, and teamwork required in both professions, and how "you don't really realize you're learning all this stuff when you're playing football because you're just playing." Mark discussed the "subconscious stuff" he learned playing college football, and how he now better understands and appreciates what his coaches were doing when they put "big words" like "resiliency" up on the monitor during those many practice meetings his teammates and he did not necessarily want to be sitting in early in the morning. Now being in the acting business, he could finally relate to what they were talking about. He has been able to transfer this mental toughness, resiliency, and other critical attributes from the sport context to his new career path.

Mark noted that playing college football has "developed me as a man" and helped him realize how much stronger he is than many other aspiring actors who give up when things do not go their way in this business. He particularly spoke about the "mental toughness" he developed playing college and professional football, and how it has helped separate him from some of his peers in acting:

It's the mental toughness, because you realize, you see a lot of people . . . will break after their first bad thing happens. They give up. So I'm like, "You're giving up?" I'm like, "What are you doing?" . . . It's kind of like, it's like we're in the second quarter and you drop a pass, and you're, like, 'I don't want to play no more.' We're in the middle of the game. Why are you giving up right now?"

When Mark and I reflected on our 2002 conversations, the issue of athlete compensation came back up. Similar to Bobby, Mark acknowledged the value of the athletic scholarship, but made it clear that contrary to popular belief of fans, students, media, and other outsiders, the athletic scholarship does not always fully cover the basic needs of college athletes, particularly Black athletes who come from low socioeconomic backgrounds. In Mark's words,

Yeah, you got a place to sleep; you got a dorm room; you got books and everything, but how are you going to eat? How are these guys going to eat?

Mark bemoaned the reality that for many Black athletes, it can be a struggle to get enough food to eat during a typical week because they don't always have the money, and in many cases, they are not able to rely on their parents or family to send them care packages with food and other essentials. Mark pointed out the discrepancies and hypocrisy in the NCAA's governance over this matter when he stated, "You mean to tell me, all this money and this revenue coming into the NCAA and you're, like, some of these guys can barely even eat." This particular issue was thrust into the national spotlight after the 2014 NCAA men's basketball national championship game when during a post-game interview, University of Connecticut player Shabazz Napier revealed that there had been many nights during his college basketball career that he went to bed hungry because he did not have the money for food. Napier's comments helped move the NCAA to approve a rule that allows Division I schools to provide unlimited meals and snacks to athletes, but they also reignited debates regarding the issue of college athletes' rights and the NCAA's inequitable policies on athlete compensation. Contributors to Eddie Comeaux's book *College Athletes' Rights and Well-Being* critically address the issue of athlete compensation and other important policy and practical matters.[19]

When asked to compare the prevalent education matters facing Black male college athletes in 2002 with those of Black male college athletes today, Mark again brought up the issue of economic exploitation and athlete compensation. He was critical about how the NCAA, the schools, and coaches are making money off the labor of these athletes, while "these random laws and like rules the NCAA creates" continue to create difficult or less than favorable educational experiences for Black male college athletes and their peers. Mark expressed frustration with the amount of money these schools are raking in today, but was particularly astounded by today's massive coaching contracts, including those of assistant coaches who "are getting a million dollars a year." Texas A&M University's fully guaranteed, ten-year, $75 million contract with new head football coach Jimbo Fisher in late 2017, and the contract that pays his defensive coordinator, Mike Elko, close to $2 million a year are a case in point.

In addition to these huge salaries for coaches, Mark was also disturbed by how much power coaches have over athletes today, and the freedom coaches have "to leave whenever they want and sign another multimillion-dollar contract at another school without having to sit out for a year or something." Athletes do not have that kind of latitude when it comes to leaving a school and being eligible to play right away at another school. Mark also discussed how coaches "can create or destroy a college player's life, their career—not just life, but career." He shared an example from his playing days. One of his teammates "did just fine in school and never got in trouble," but because the coaches did not like his "jokester" personality, they never gave him the opportunity to play, even though "he was a phenomenal athlete" who "could easily have been playing on Sundays." (Playing on Sundays, the day most games are played in the NFL, means a player has reached the pinnacle in the most popular and financially successful sport league in the US). At the time I was finishing this book, the NCAA had revisited and begun making some changes to its transfer rules; for example, athletes no longer need permission from schools to seek transfers. But critics point out that football and basketball athletes still have to sit out a year in many cases and there are still too many loopholes in the rules that leave athletes vulnerable to retaliation from schools and coaches, including canceling their scholarships, if they decide to pursue a better situation.[20]

Mark also revisited the issue his teammates and he discussed in 2002 about the negative stereotypes of Black quarterbacks and Black male athletes in general being "categorized as a certain type of athlete" in comparison with their White counterparts. He recalled a time where the coaching staff brought a Black quarterback and White quarterback into the program in the same recruiting class, and although from his perspective, the Black athlete was the "superior" quarterback, the coaching staff labeled his position as "athlete." Mark expressed his bewilderment with this decision:

> They didn't have him as quarterback. I'm, like, this guy is a quarterback. . . I remember at one point, they had him doing kickoff returns. I'm like, "You have a quarterback doing kickoff returns. He's the better athlete, he's the better quarterback. I don't understand." But . . . it's the weirdest thing, if you're a Black quarterback, they just think that you're going to be running the whole time, like you're not smart enough to be able to control offense . . . These are the worst . . . stereotypes, and you can see them like boldface, like right in your face.

Mark's critical reflection on this example of how one Black quarterback was handled by the coaching staff helps further explain and clarify why his teammates and he viewed access discrimination against Black athletes in the quarterback position as a matter of racism in college sport during their playing days.

One final thing that came up in our discussion of differences between the then and now for Black male college athletes was the issue of social media in the era of the Black Lives Matter movement. Mark discussed the exposure and scrutiny today's Black athlete is faced with compared with what his peers and he faced when he played, before the rise and popularity of social media. He specifically broached the subject of the national anthem controversy sparked by Colin Kaepernick, and acknowledged that "we didn't have to deal with" the backlash and overt racism on Twitter, Facebook and other social media that Black athletes now face when they decide to use their platform to challenge racial injustice:

> I can only imagine the pressure and the feeling of . . . especially a college athlete, where you're on a scholarship and the coaches control everything. You don't have the power of, like, an NFL guy where say you're a superstar and you could have a little bit more of a leeway, could have more of a voice. You can't have no voice; they can muzzle you quickly in college . . . by threatening you with not playing . . . or

getting on the field just because you want to speak your mind on . . . justice . . . So that's the thing that always hits me where I'm, like, man, that's the total difference from now and then when I played.

Mark believed college athletes in this fourth wave of athlete activism should be able to speak up and speak out against injustice, but he acknowledged that given the sociopolitical climate of this era, Black male athletes must "realize there might be some blowback, and you've got to be prepared for that."

As we concluded our interview, Mark offered his thoughts on Black male athlete education matters going forward. In particular, he shared how he wishes that he would have taken more risks in pursuit of "something that's maybe not the norm." Although he acknowledged that both his parents being educators influenced his decision to pursue an education degree as a college athlete, Mark suggested he might have been better prepared for his career in acting and the film industry had he done something different and pursued a degree in film studies instead. He revisited the conversation his teammates and he had in 2002 about how Black male athletes "get funneled" or clustered into certain courses and academic majors by academic advisers because of the perception that these courses and majors are deemed to be easy for these athletes. Therefore, Mark's recommendation to "my twenty-one-year old self" and Black male athletes in the present and future is to "take more control of what you want" and not allow academic advisers and other people to limit their pursuit of different educational experiences.

Marcus

Unlike with Bobby and Mark, I was unfortunately unable to catch up with Marcus in 2018 for a follow-up conversation. However, through my conversations with Bobby and Mark and other important secondary sources of information, I was able to gain some insight into where Marcus is now in both his career and thinking around Black male athlete education matters. In particular, I relied heavily on interviews and feature stories that journalists and other writers have done with Marcus since he retired from the NFL, along with his *Wikipedia* page and LinkedIn profiles to provide a summary of where Marcus was in life at the time I completed this book.

As of late 2018, Marcus was married with children and had worked his way up the ranks in a corporate entity in the area of sales. He also had intentions of going back to his alma mater to earn a master's degree in business. In discussing how his status as a former high-profile college athlete now working in the state where he played college football has helped him in his career after football, Marcus stated that his former athlete status certainly opened up doors of opportunity for him. But he was quick to admit that once that door is opened you must demonstrate your competence, or otherwise you will be shown the way out the door by the leaders who make the hiring decisions. When asked how he liked the career path in sales that he was on, Marcus shared how he appreciated the opportunity it afforded him to provide for his family. He acknowledged that working in corporate sales is different than playing professional sports for a living, but that he still has to have a similar mental motivation to get up and go after his goals. Marcus appears to apply the same passion he had as an athlete in his work now in corporate sales.

In reflecting on his transition from being an NFL athlete to a career in sales, Marcus spoke about the importance of Black male athletes like him having identities beyond the athlete role and status. He was very explicit in stating that if he would have allowed his identity as a football player to consume him, he might not be alive today, and probably would not have a wife and family. There is no doubt that football played an important role in his life. But Marcus was clear about his efforts to not let being a football player define who he is, and how people who really get to know him understand that he has other important identities beyond his athletic identity.

To the young athletes who see him as a role model (including his younger brother, who was competing in high school football and being recruited by top Division I programs at the time of my writing), Marcus has consistently communicated this message—that sport participation can indeed help you build character, work ethic, team camaraderie, and self-motivation, but should not define who you are.

A few years into his NFL playing career, Marcus established a charitable foundation with the goal of advancing education, particularly for underprivileged and underserved youth who come from troubled communities (including prevalent juvenile delinquency, high neighborhood tensions, prejudice and discrimination, and community deterioration). He has partnered with companies and organizations in the area where he grew up to run youth football camps, provide back to school supplies for students and gifts for children during the holidays, and serve as a motivational speaker and mentor for students in the P–12 schools. He has earned awards and recognition for his service to youth in the Black community. Although I did not hear directly from Marcus, the focal point of his foundation gives me some perspective on what his thoughts were about Black male athlete education matters in the here and now. Marcus clearly understands and is committed to the crucial role education plays in life opportunities and outcomes for young Black males and other youth.

DISCUSSION AND CONCLUSION

The narratives of Bobby, Mark, and Marcus helped illuminate some educational issues and challenges these particular Black male athletes faced as students in both high school and the big-time college football program in which they all played together in as teammates. As one of the tenets of CRT, Gloria Ladson-Billings and William Tate argued, "The voice of people of color is required for a complete analysis of the educational system."[21] Likewise, I argue here that the voice of Black male athletes is necessary to better understand and address educational challenges this particular student population faces in P–12 and higher education. The Black males viewed their participation in this case study as an important platform to voice their concerns and share their stories, and I focused on the centrality of experiential knowledge from the voices of Bobby, Mark, and Marcus to allow them to name their own realities as high profile athletes in this big-time college sport program.

The narratives that Bobby, Mark and Marcus shared are of particular importance to helping advance what is known about the educational challenges of Black male athletes. Marcus and Mark both revealed how in high school they shifted focus primarily to athletics once they realized they were talented enough to play football at the major college level. This shift to a predominant focus on sports is a familiar story for many other young Black males, past and present, who exhibit great athletic prowess during, and in some instances, even well before they reach high school. Several of the Black male athletes I worked with as an academic adviser in the SUPER program mentioned in chapter 1 shared with me how they did not take academics seriously and focused more on athletics during high school. Some shared stories of how teachers and other educational stakeholders such as coaches and school administrators had low expectations for their academic performance, often allowing them to miss class with few or no consequences. Marcus, Mark, and other Black male athletes I have worked with throughout the years acknowledged some culpability for their academic underperformance in high school. However, their stories also point to issues at meso-level cultures of low academic expectations in P–12 schools that often negatively affect Black male athletes once they reach HWCU.

Bobby's story of academic success in high school serves as an important counter-narrative to the popular discourse on the chronic academic underperformance of Black male athletes. Unfortunately, one limitation of this case study is I did not delve deeply enough into Bobby's or Marcus's and Mark's P–12 histories and backgrounds to know the extent to which they might have been impacted by the culture of low academic expectations that could have existed in their respective high school and P–8 experiences. Despite this limitation, Bobby's narrative challenges the Black "dumb jock" myth and other racial stereotypes (e.g., deficient, disengaged, apathetic) aimed at Black male athletes.[22]

This case study also contributes to the ongoing dialogue concerning the educational experiences and challenges of Black male college athletes. Kristen Benson's narratives of the schooling experiences of "at-risk" African American male college athletes was one of the first early studies that encouraged these athletes to "name their own reality."[23] This current study was concerned not only with Bobby, Marcus, and Mark's narratives about their schooling experiences but also about what the concept of education means to them. Bobby echoed the sentiments of Harry Edwards in his acknowledgment that graduation is not equivalent to education, and being educated goes well beyond getting good grades and earning a college degree.[24] It also entails gaining knowledge of who you are as a person, and learning about the world and people from different backgrounds. In a similar vein, Mark viewed education as learning how to be independent and deal with "real life" issues.

From a CRT perspective, Marcus's conception of education was particularly insightful because he inferred that race was significant when he suggested that Black male athletes must be culturally versed in the norms and realities of their own communities, as well as White mainstream society in order to be educated. Marcus was keenly aware that racism is embedded in the US educational system and that Black people are not being holistically educated in the current system but are being trained to conform to the cultural orientations of White elites. Marcus saw his development as moving beyond the limitations of the Eurocentric ways of thinking and knowing and embracing and directly confronting the challenges and circumstances he experienced as a Black male athlete at a HWCU. To him, education was about garnering an understanding of "the world and everything around you," and eventually maturing into an independent and self-sufficient Black man.

During our initial focus group discussion, Bobby, Mark, and Marcus initiated a conversation around racism. Both Bobby and Mark expressed an awareness of how racial stereotypes by university educational stakeholders can lead to treatment discrimination against African American male athletes. They alluded to college professors who unfairly judge Black male athletes and label them as lazy, troublemakers, and not serious students, partially because of their distinctive skin color, height and size, and clothing. They also shared how White academic support staff within the athletic department attempt to schedule Black male athletes for classes they do not need to take, but give the White athletes classes that advance them toward graduation. However, in line with CRT, Bobby, Mark, and Marcus countered this treatment discrimination by choosing their own class schedules and/or going to the Black academic support staff to help them with their class schedules.

Mark's story of his "real dark" teammate who was seemingly always selected for "random" drug testing is another example of how racial stereotypes lead to treatment discrimination against Black male athletes. Mark perceived that some of his White teammates seemed not to face any real consequences for their wrongdoing. Mark suggested that Black athletes, whether guilty or not of some indiscretion or transgression, do not typically get the same benefit of the doubt or second chances their White counterparts often enjoy. This is an example of the privileges associated with Whiteness that CRT and other scholars have discussed in the literature.[25] Bobby and Mark's examples demonstrate how White privilege can account for the unequal educational opportunities available to athletes from different races, and treatment discrimination can adversely impact the educational experiences and outcomes of Black male athletes.

The Black males in this study also shared stories about access discrimination. Marcus and Mark both expressed how Black athletes have taken over and dominated the fields and courts of play at HWCU, but opportunities at the top of the organizational hierarchy have been severely limited for Black athletes. Marcus suggested that progress has been made with regard to more Black athletes playing the quarterback position. However, the long-held racial stereotype that they lack the mental capacity to play the position are still around and have limited Black athletes' full access to this leadership position on the field.[26] We have seen more Black male college athletes in the quarterback position since this study was conducted in 2002. However, they still often contend with the racial stereotype they are athletically superior while intellectually inferior to White male athletes.[27]

Marcus and Mark also discussed the access discrimination Black males experience when pursuing head coaching and upper management careers in college and professional sport. Mark suggested Black males must achieve exceptional, extraordinary feats on the field of play as athletes to even be considered for such positions; and in many cases, this still is not enough for them to be hired into these major decision-making, leadership positions. My colleagues and I and other scholars have drawn from CRT and other relevant theories to examine the dearth of Blacks in these leadership positions.[28] We found in our reanalysis of the measures used from the Black Coaches and Administrators (BCA) Hiring Report Card to assess the hiring process of NCAA athletic departments that *process racism*, which Molefi Asante described as procedures that produce racially disparate outcomes, was a major factor in the pervasive denial of Black males' access to head football coaching opportunities.[29] This is one of the reasons Bobby, Mark, and Marcus stressed the need for more Black people in influential positions of leadership within HWCU and their athletics departments.

As another way to help bring about institutional integrity in college sport at HWCU, Bobby, Mark, and Marcus expressed the need for a more equitable distribution of the financial resources that are largely generated by their labor. They were quite disgruntled by the huge disparities that exist between what athletes receive and what coaches and other employees in college sport receive. These Black males understood that this hypocritical system, created by and for elite White males is highly corrupt, dishonest, and ultimately, unsustainable. Their narratives challenged the "amateur myth" that Allen Sack and Ellen Staurowsky interrogated in their 1998 book, *College Athletes for Hire*.[30]

Despite the injustice that continues to exist in college sport, Bobby, Mark, and Marcus acknowledged college sport did provide financial, psychological, and social benefits during and after their participation. While some of the policies and the extreme time demands associated with their roles restricted these benefits during their time as athletes, each of them realized that playing major college football afforded them transferable skills that they have been able to apply to their post-playing career paths. For example, Bobby and Mark drew parallels between the challenges associated with playing college football and breaking into and being successful in their acting careers.

In conclusion, Joseph Cooper's excellence beyond athletics framework has relevance for this case study. I stress here the importance of college sport and higher education stakeholders, including the athletes themselves, paying attention to and implementing some of the best practices—self-identity awareness, positive social engagement, active mentorship, academic achievement, career aspirations, and balanced time management—that Cooper advanced in this framework.[31] Similar to what Harry Edwards has asserted, Cooper has argued that Black athletes must ultimately hold themselves accountable for their own educational experiences and outcomes. As mentioned earlier, Cooper suggested these athletes do this by strategically responding to interest convergence (SRIC) in this exploitative college sport system. The SRIC approach posits three necessary attributes. First is *holistic consciousness*; that is, Black athletes must recognize the inequitable structural arrangement that is designed to exploit them. The Black male athletes featured in this case study demonstrated a holistic consciousness by recognizing the impact the inordinate time spent in athletics had on other developmentally useful activities outside of sport participation, and the disparities in financial compensation between athletes and other stakeholders. Second, *internalized empowerment* refers to how Black athletes must internalize or believe they possess the power to alter their personal outcomes within this system. Bobby, Marcus, and Mark all demonstrated this empowerment by using the challenges they faced on the field as a mechanism to develop and deal with challenges off the field. Finally, Black athletes must *engage in counter-actions*, or actively push back against the inequitable arrangements to maximize the holistic benefits for themselves, which these athletes did by not allowing white academic counselors to choose their schedules. I further discuss some of the issues raised in this chapter in chapter 4.

CHAPTER 3

Individual Narratives on Black Male Athlete Excellence and Resilience

Stop treating us like we're stupid . . . It takes a lot of intelligence to play sports, especially football.

Willis

Meet the student [athlete] where he or she is at . . . maybe they're not good at certain things, but find out what they are good at and try to tailor a program around their strengths.

John

How easy is it to get everybody [college athletes] across the stage [graduation] with a 2.0 . . . How hard is it to get across the stage with how to use a 2.0 to change the world?

Marc

I N THIS CHAPTER, I present individual narrative vignettes that provide powerful snapshots into the educational experiences and outcomes of nine former Black male college athletes who participated in football at Division I HWCU. (One of the athletes featured in this chapter played both football and basketball during his time as a college athlete.) The vignettes also offer insight into these athletes' broader perspectives on Black male athlete education matters and recommendations they offer toward improving the educational circumstances of Black male athletes at Division I HWCU. Although the primary focus of this chapter is on these nine Black males' college sport experiences and its aftermath, I do provide insight into how some of their P–12 schooling, home life, upbringing, and other pre-college experiences prepared them for college sport participation. It is my hope that the inclusion of such information will provide important context for readers to better appreciate the educational experiences and outcomes of these Black males.

METHODOLOGY

In deciding on whom to feature in this chapter, I initially relied on my personal and professional contacts with former Black male college athletes as well as recommendations from others who also had such contacts. In addition, I took a snowball sampling approach by soliciting recommendations from some of the athletes who originally agreed to share their stories for this chapter. To construct the vignettes, I drew from semistructured individual interviews I conducted face to face or via telephone with seven of these former athletes and received written narratives from the other two, who responded directly to a series of interview guide questions.

In general, I asked each of these Black males to respond to questions regarding:

- Their initial thoughts on the topic of Black male athlete education matters
- P–12 schooling and early sport experiences
- Their conceptions and definitions of education
- External and internal factors they deemed to have impacted their education and the education of Black male athletes more generally
- Recommendations to improve the educational experiences and outcomes of Black male college athletes

The primary data that emerged from these interviews was augmented by news articles and feature stories, social media accounts, personal and professional websites, university athletic department websites, and other secondary sources. In addition, each participant filled out a questionnaire that provided demographic and other relevant information. They each chose a pseudonym to mask their identities (although one of them chose to use his actual first name).

My analysis of the data involved a general inductive process.[1] This included a detailed reading of the transcripts of the recorded interviews and the written narratives, my field notes, and relevant artifacts of communication. Once I constructed the initial vignettes, I sent each participant my working draft of his vignette for review and feedback. I also engaged each in follow-up phone or email conversations about my interpretations of their words and sentiments. For the most part, all nine participants were pleased with my initial (re)presentation of their stories and perspectives, although in a few cases, some did suggest that I delete or reframe certain passages that might give away their identity or be misconstrued by readers. In a few instances, they provided additional clarifying context and/or commentary. My engagement in follow-up communication was essential to the process of co-creating the knowledge that is shared below.

SHEDRICK: FROM STUDENT IN SPECIAL EDUCATION TO COLLEGIATE SCHOLAR ATHLETE OF THE YEAR

One day I was approached by a coach about a couple of student-athletes who were not doing well academically and had a poor academic background. I had these student-athletes set up for success . . . I helped them select classes that most students across campus were successful in. I had them meeting with reading specialists, learning specialists, and tutors and spending countless hours in study hall, but they still were struggling. I asked the coach a question and gave him a scenario: "Let's say I was a coach for a season and I recruited all Academic All-Americans, but they played basketball on the fourth- and fifth-grade level . . . meaning I'm having to teach them how to shoot free throws, dribble, and do layups. How many games will we win? Probably not many. But, academically they're performing very well." This is the same thing I'm having to deal with in the classroom, when student-athletes are not performing well academically . . . I'm/we're having to teach them the fundamentals of education. Again, those student-athletes were not dumb at all; they just had to play catch-up academically to be successful in the classroom because someone along the way should have been taking more responsibility helping those students be successful in the classroom.

This is how Shedrick answered my question about the responsibility educational stakeholders in both P–12 and higher education have for the educational experiences of college athletes. The conversation he recounts took place when he was an academic adviser for men's basketball at a major

Division I HWCU. The hypothetical scenario he offered was prompted by his experiences working "with student-athletes in the past that read on the fourth- and fifth-grade level, but were accepted into Tier 1 institutions." Reflecting on his own educational experiences and outcomes and those of other Black male college athletes, Shedrick was strongly convinced that "It's never the case where a student-athlete is dumb or not smart enough." Rather, it has more to do with teachers, coaches, principals, and others in the P–12 educational system "who just passed the student along because of their ability to play their sport well enough." To Shedrick's point, there are numerous documented cases where highly talented Black male football and basketball athletes have been recruited out of the P–12 educational system into major HWCU to play football and basketball in particular, even though poor academic preparation set them up for limited success in higher education. (For example, education scholar Jamel Donnor discussed the case of Kevin Ross, a former Marquette University basketball player whose reading and language skills were so underdeveloped when he was recruited and offered an athletic scholarship to the university that after his four years of eligibility expired, he ended up attending Chicago's Westside Preparatory School (K–8) for remedial education.[2])

Shedrick grew up in a single-parent home with his mother and siblings in a small, predominantly White Southwestern town. Regarding his P–12 schooling, Shedrick wrote, "I was not a good student throughout elementary school, due to not having a good attitude towards school, and anger issues. Let's just say I was bad." Shedrick attributed his behavior mostly to his parents getting a divorce when he was young. While he was honest about how he "stayed in and out of trouble" during his early elementary schooling, he made it clear that "it was never the case of me not being smart enough, but had everything to do with my bad behavior and bad attitude." He shared how these issues and his not taking school seriously led to him being "placed in special education classes and told by some educators that I would be a special education student until I graduated high school—that's if I graduated."

The turning point for Shedrick came around the third or fourth grade, when two special education educators (a Black female and Black male) "took me under their wings and helped mold me to become a great student":

These two individuals knew that I was more than capable of being successful academically. Therefore, they challenged me academically and they also knew how to get through to me. I grew to respect them greatly, which caused my attitude to change towards my education in a positive way. They taught me how to read, write, and do math. By the time I was placed back into the "normal" classroom setting, I was more advanced than many in my class.

In follow-up conversations, Shedrick shared with me how it was the female teacher—to whom he had a previous personal connection through family members—who first let him know she wanted to help him succeed. From the moment Shedrick stepped into her classroom, he "felt the love" and "that she cared" about him. When he transitioned to the sixth grade, the Black male special education teacher continued the good work. According to Shedrick, this educator let him know that he did not belong in special education, but since he was in his class, he was going to use it as an opportunity to teach Shedrick everything he needed to know to move forward. It was this teacher who taught him how to use reflective journal writing to channel his anger. Doing so helped him begin to channel his anger on the football field instead of in the classroom. Shedrick largely credits these teachers with putting him on the right track to graduating from high school and eventually earning his bachelor's and master's degrees.

Shedrick enjoyed learning and participating in football, basketball, and track and field during his P–12 schooling. As a young Black male who excelled in football in a state where high school football is treated like a religion, Shedrick was heavily recruited by several major Division I football programs. He decided to accept a scholarship to play defensive back at a large state university in the South that is affiliated with arguably the top FBS conference in the nation. He expressed his gratitude for the opportunity this scholarship afforded him to attend college, "because otherwise my family was not financially able to send me to college."

Shedrick, who graduated from college with over a 3.0 GPA and was scholar-athlete of the year during his senior year, also acknowledged that participating in college sport taught him "a lot of life lessons." He discussed how playing college football taught him the value of paying greater attention to detail and avoiding unnecessary and potentially costly mistakes in life. More specifically, he shared how his coaches would correlate making mistakes on the football field with mistakes in life, and that being more diligent about avoiding such errors could translate to making sound decisions in life. He also shared how having to juggle the the packed itinerary of a college football athlete taught him the values of "hard work," "work ethic," and "discipline" and how this has actually helped him better manage his work-life balance and get the most out of his day-to-day life activities.

Shedrick noted how because college sport is "run like a business," it places more demands on college athletes' time—to the point where "it is impossible to study twenty-four to thirty-six hours per week" as higher education professionals suggest. According to Shedrick "every day, your schedule looks like an itinerary" and "playing a sport at a D-I [Division I] institution and going to school full-time can take up . . . sixty-six hours or more a week." He asserted that poor time management can "easily hinder your performance on the field or in the classroom." Similar to the Black male athletes featured in chapter 2, Shedrick perceived that the struggle to manage the competing time demands of playing big-time college football and trying to engage in other developmentally useful activities outside of football is a real detriment.

Also like Bobby, Mark, and Marcus in chapter 2, Shedrick acknowledged that racial stereotypes had an impact on his educational experiences:

> Students and professors of different races sometimes felt you were only on campus and attending school because you were an athlete. Most felt that because they had to work hard academically to get into school—the student-athletes got in by other standards (NCAA standards), which are lower—so some viewed student-athletes differently.

Shedrick was also asked to reflect broadly on how various matters at the societal, institutional/organizational, and individual levels might have influenced his and his peers' educational experiences and outcomes. Initially, he implied that the athlete seasoning complex (see chapter 1) is an important matter that can have a negative effect on the education of college athletes:

> Many student-athletes will tell you that as a child, they were told by family members, friends, and community leaders that they were going to play in the NBA or the NFL when they got older . . . Hardly anyone was asking them what they are going to major in. It was as if [these people] were only excited about how many touchdowns were scored on Friday nights or how many baskets were scored during a basketball game. So with that being said, that starts a paradigm shift. Many

student-athletes when they were younger believed that they were going to the "league" and because of that some didn't take their education [seriously]. I call this the "dirty trick."

This notion of the "dirty trick" is the same term that sociologist Reuben May used in his book *Living Through the Hoop* to describe the influence media, coaches, community, and individual athletes' mind-sets have in convincing young Black males that sport participation is the most effective path to upward social mobility.[3] Shedrick was keenly aware of the "dirty trick" the athlete seasoning complex played on far too many young Black males, and the deleterious influence it had on their education as college athletes.

Shedrick also wrote about how particular matters at the micro or individual level contribute to Black male athletes' education. He emphasized how college athletes' attitudes, goals, aspirations, and behaviors are all essential to their success as students:

> If you're only focused on your sport and playing professionally, then as a student athlete, you may only do enough to get by academically. Meaning, you may only do enough to be eligible by the NCAA to play, and this sometimes means not graduating.

Shedrick provided insight into his own "mind-set of working hard on and off the field" during his college playing days, and his mind-set and decision-making regarding his future beyond a career playing football. Unlike many of his teammates who didn't finish their degrees and found it difficult to return to college after pursuing an NFL playing career, Shedrick prioritized his schooling and formal education over the pursuit of a professional playing career:

> After graduating with my bachelor's degree, our associate athletic director approached me about a graduate assistantship, but I told her I needed some time to think about it because I had other opportunities at the time, such as working in law enforcement and/or working out for the NFL draft. Since the NFL wasn't promised and [I was] dealing with [shoulder surgeries], I decided to pass on that opportunity, which many thought I was crazy for doing. There was no doubt in my mind that I would have done well enough during my workouts and

would have gotten a free agency deal because I've always tested well and exceeded these test/drills since I was a true freshmen in college (40-yard dash, bench press, vertical jump, broad jump, L drill, etc.). Instead, I decided to attend graduate school and work as a graduate assistant, which was the best decision I could have made and I don't regret none of it. I was able to leave school with my master's degree and have zero debt as a result, meaning I didn't owe anyone anything.

Shedrick's lived experiences as a Division I college football athlete, academic adviser for athletics at a major Division I university, and, at the time of this writing, an academic adviser for the general student population at another major HWCU informed his perspectives on what Black male athletes should do to enhance their own educational experiences and outcomes. He strongly believes college athletes "should always take control over their own educational experience" and not allow athletic academic staff or coaches to choose their academic majors for them. He also insisted on the need for these athletes to "understand their degree plan and why they're taking the classes they're taking," and "take classes that are going to set you up for success and challenge you . . . in your chosen field of study." In his concluding thoughts on Black male athlete education matters, Shedrick shared how he took individual responsibility and used challenges he faced as a college athlete to help mold and shape him into a better person and professional in his post-playing life:

> I was able to take on the responsibility of raising a young family (had a daughter my sophomore year in college) . . . I moved my child and the mother of my children in with me. Being a student athlete was challenging enough, but raising a small family on top of being a student-athlete made things more challenging. Those responsibilities helped mold me into the person/professional I am today.

LAWRENCE: PUBLISHED AUTHOR AND ASPIRING DIVISION I COLLEGIATE ATHLETIC DIRECTOR

As an African American male, I can say freely that there is a perception that everyone is going to the NFL, which stands for "not for long." There is a lot of outside pressure from family members and other stakeholders in their [Black male athletes'] lives to make it. We really need to make a concerted effort to break this stigma in order to be successful.

This quote demonstrates that, like Shedrick, Lawrence was keenly aware of the negative impact the athlete seasoning complex can have on the education of Black male athletes. At the time Lawrence provided his written narrative, he was a twenty-nine-year-old director of football advising at a major HWCU (not the one where he had played college football). He had also just started working toward his MBA degree because he recognized how much of a business college sport has become today. He has a professional goal to one day "become the youngest AD [athletic director] in D-1 collegiate athletics" and he wanted to enhance his business acumen.

Like many young Black males, Lawrence was introduced to football by his family, particularly his father, and very early on showed a strong affinity for the game. However, his narrative on his P–12 experiences makes it clear that although he and his family had strong aspirations for him to play college football and nurtured that goal, his schooling and overall educational experiences prepared him well for the academic rigors of college and success beyond the playing field:

> From 3K [sic] to tenth grade, I attended a private school . . . my parents sacrificed a lot for me to attend so I could enhance my skills, and to be in a place where I can discuss my faith freely. After my tenth-grade year, I begged my parents to allow me to attend ["football juggernaut" high school] to see how good I was and to gain more exposure from collegiate coaches. The private school was predominately a Caucasian school, where [the other school] was more diverse. Both schools were located in fairly good places in town where it was safe to attend, and you did not have to worry about many bad things occurring. I was fortunate that both schools had great resources, and I was challenged with a plethora of AP courses and college prep work to prepare me for college. The private school was a smaller juggernaut with great sports programs, but the other school was the mecca of sports programs in [name of city] and that's why I convinced my parents to let me attend.

Lawrence's faith was very important to him, and the prestigious private school he attended for most of his P–12 schooling was a Christian school.

But from a sport perspective, it was important for him to transfer to the "football juggernaut" public high school for his final two years to elevate his chances of securing a Division I football scholarship.

Lawrence described himself as a "very strong student in high school" who graduated with close to a 3.7 GPA. Although he "was a bright young man," he did admit that he struggled with standardized test taking, but "was able to seek support from my parents to help provide tutors to help me improve my scores." Lawrence was offered a football scholarship to play defensive back at a HWCU in one of the programs affiliated with an FBS power five conference. In reflecting on how his college playing career influenced his education, Lawrence stated, "It played a vital role in my life, and helped provide structure to my life which I still currently live by." He further elaborated on how college sport participation enhanced his learning and educational opportunities:

> [I]n order to separate yourself in football, you are required to be a student of the game. Being able to analyze film, and break it down truly is a skill because you go the extra-mile to be the best. Those transferable skills translate to the classroom because there is a direct correlation to being successful on both sides.

Many scholars who study college sport and practitioners who have worked in this context would agree with Lawrence.

Although Lawrence identified as an African American male, he did not think race really mattered in regard to his personal educational experiences as a college athlete. But in reflecting on broader issues in US society and the effect they have on college athletes' education, he did acknowledge that "the educational system across the country is struggling because there are many students that are not equipped to be in school." Lawrence gave the specific example of how "many students are underprepared and have not been challenged in high school so they struggle to make a successful transition into college." As mentioned in chapter 1, many of these students are Black males who are recruited and admitted into HWCU specifically to play football and basketball. This is one of the reasons why during his time as a master's student and graduate assistant in athletics at the university where he played football, Lawrence developed and administered a freshman mentoring program to help get football athletes acclimated to college and learn essential life skills. It is also one of the reasons why he and a former college teammate (also a Black male) coauthored and published a book that focused on helping prospective and current college athletes successfully transition into and out of college sport, and navigate their way through college sport both on and off the field.

In offering his final thoughts on the role of college sport in the education of athletes, Lawrence stated:

> It is imperative that student-athletes take advantage of everything the university has to offer. Personally, I did not have a vested interest in the university until my junior year, but I should have had more of a pulse on things that were going on campus and other things that could have given me access to key stakeholders or donors. Carpe diem and make every day count is what I tell all my students.

JAMES C.: WALK-ON WITH LEARNING DISABILITY TURNED PHD SCHOLAR-ATHLETE

So in the high school context, I said football saved me. In my college experience, I would say football made me. It made me who I am today, because it gave me a process to decision making. It gave me a framework of how to approach problems. It gave me a framework of how to prepare. It gave me a framework of how to interact in high-pressure situations and how to adjust and adapt, how to quite frankly get punched in the mouth and get back up. All these things that you only can learn through experience. You can't read a book on resilience and all [of a] sudden become resilient. You got to go through something.

The quote above is a powerful expression of James's perspective on the nexus of his sport participation and educational outcomes. This twenty-three-year old former college athlete had studied abroad and was an entrepreneur, student development professional, and learning science researcher at the time of our interview. James had been a walk-on-turned-scholarship athlete who had played defensive back and on special teams in football programs at two different FBS conference–affiliated schools. It became clear in our conversations that football contributed greatly to his education and the path he is now on in life. James challenged the view that education is simply the acquisition and application of knowledge, declaring, "I am always in the classroom . . . I have never moved out of the classroom." His view of the world is that every situation you encounter in life, particularly outside the formal classroom setting, provides an opportunity to learn life lessons, and playing sports helped him really understand this.

In discussing his early schooling experiences, James shared that he "actually struggled a lot in preK–12." He provided some very insightful commentary about a learning disability that challenged him during his P–12 schooling and that went undiagnosed until he was well into college:

> I had actually undiagnosed learning disabilities, didn't get diagnosed with dyslexia until I was twenty-one. So I struggled in elementary school, middle school, high school. Struggled with coursework because I got bored easily, one, and frustrated with myself because I wasn't sure what my learning style was; so I struggled with retaining information and I would consistently forget content, forget information that was covered. And so I was labeled as one of those low academic achievers and just kids who cared about their sport, not about school. And especially when I got to high school, was pretty much dismissed by teachers and almost didn't graduate high school, which is crazy now that I think about it . . . I failed English class twice, so I had to repeat freshman English and repeat sophomore English because I really struggled with grammar. And that was back when I didn't understand how I learned.

Interestingly, his further commentary on these learning challenges demonstrated the real potential of sport to help him navigate his undiagnosed disability. According to James, "Honestly, what saved me was football. One, I had to be eligible to play, but then two, because it gave me structure and something to shoot for and it was my outlet." When asked to describe what dyslexia was and how football helped him combat this learning disability, James offered the following response:

> In layman terms, basically my brain moves faster than my mouth. So I struggle with articulating what I'm thinking, and then also word associations. Meanings of words and what they mean to me, I struggle with. Memorization (and spelling) falls into that category. So how football saves me and how football actually helped my learning is I

had to memorize the playbook. And I had to memorize defensive calls and defensive concepts, and when the coach gave the signal, I had to do that on the field in order to be successful. And so through that, I learned how I learned. And basically implemented that into my studies once I got to college, and the rest is history.

This narrative is a powerful revelation about the pivotal role high school football played in helping him figure out his learning style and in the process elevate himself both on and off the field going forward.

James's experiences as an unheralded high school football athlete with a learning disability prompted him to become "hyper-focused on proving people wrong" as he transitioned into college and pursued opportunities as a football walk-on in his first year at a major Division I university. He had some interest from Division II schools and one Division IAA school, but because James was "this stubborn eighteen-year-old kid" who wanted to play Division I and get a great college experience, he emailed and called every single Division I school "begging them to ask me to try out." Only six of the roughly 120 schools responded, and two confirmed or guaranteed him a tryout. James decided to go to the one that was relatively close to home. Self-described as a "human tackling dummy" during his freshman year, James often questioned why he was there, especially considering that one of the coaches told him before he ever got to the university that he would never play there. But he persisted and went from being a walk-on to a starting safety. James played his final year in that program under a different head coach because the head coach (a Black male) who was there when he first got to that HWCU had taken a head coaching job at another FBS school. Therefore, after graduating early in just under three years, James decided to transfer to another FBS school. Although he acknowledged it was a hard decision for him, James did it because he "had really grown in my self-awareness and what I wanted out of life, and I just didn't agree with the way that [new] head coach was running the program."

In choosing his next institution to play football as a graduate transfer with two years of eligibility remaining, James really focused on major Tier 1 research universities and their academic prestige. It was at this point that James was first exposed to the harsh realities of Division I college sport being a big business:

> [I]t's crazy, this is how I found out about the business of college sports.
> I was planning to go to the [name of university] and had taken the GRE
> twice . . . while I was in spring practice, took it, got a good enough
> score, got accepted into [name of university] on my own without the
> help of the athletic department, and then had the opportunity to trans-
> fer there and go play football for [name of university]. It ended up not
> working out. They ended up taking another graduate transfer instead
> of me, basically a week before I was planning to move up there.

Fortunately, James was able to land on his feet and play football as a graduate transfer walk-on at a comparable peer institution in the same athletic
conference as the one that made the "business" decision to take the other
transfer.

Although his playing career at this new institution never really panned
out, due at least in part to foot injuries, James viewed his decision to transfer
as "the best decision I ever made because now, looking back, it gave me a
whole new network and a whole new frame of reference on what elite performance is." He was able to complete his master's degree in one year, and
begin doctoral studies while still playing football during his final year of
eligibility, making him one of the few, if not only, Division I college football or basketball athletes to pursue a doctoral degree while still playing
his sport.

Reflecting on how potential external and internal matters might have
impacted his education, James provided some interesting insight into the
bubble that big-time college football often places college athletes in. He
shared an example of a time when a major incident on campus gained
national media attention. It was traumatic for many students and the campus community at large. Despite this situation, "we had football practice
the exact same day. Coach never brought it up, and acted like nothing happened . . . So that happened on campus; there's students who are scarred
and may have post-traumatic stress over that, and we're going to practice
because we got to play." This is a poignant example of the all-too-common
reality of how big-time college sport often neglects the social and emotional
needs of athletes as students in the larger social contexts outside their football and basketball programs.

James also talked about the low academic expectations that are placed
on athletes like him in big-time college sport programs:

I think just the lower expectation placed upon athletes academically. There's one very vivid example in my mind; again [year] was probably the most important year academically for me, the first semester of the PhD . . . At the time I was writing about student-athlete mental health, and I'm drawing an entire educational model and pulling from different theories and writing a solid twenty-five-page manuscript. And I'm trying to help create change on campus. And one of the academic advisers within athletics came up to me and said "James, you've already done enough . . . you don't need to do that. Why are you doing that?" And I was like "Wow, what do you mean?" He's like, "You know you're the first PhD student" . . . I'm like "That's not important to me. It's important to me to create change. That's why I'm doing the PhD." And so the fact that, again, this person works for the university, for the athletic department, as an adviser telling me to stop, in a sense, what I was doing . . . it was just eye-opening to me that, one, that took place, but then two, no one expected me to give back or contribute back. That was never . . . tied in to what I was doing. It was more like, "Hey, you did it, you graduated, now get out of here."

James was taken aback by this athletic academic adviser suggesting he should tone down or even completely abandon his scholarly work. This propensity for some educational stakeholders in athletic departments to discourage athletes from pursuing educational goals and activities beyond sport participation corresponds with Eddie Comeaux's work on the cultures of low academic expectations that are embedded in major athletic departments at HWCU.[4]

In regard to internal matters that had an impact on his educational experiences as a college athlete, James provided a fascinating example of how the pressure to perform on the big stage that is major college sport can negatively impact the mental state of individual athletes:

We had a game against [name of the conference opponent] and I had worked so hard to that point to get playing time. I ended up playing in the game and on my third play . . . I give up a touchdown on national television. And to say I was in a bad mental state is an understatement . . . I actually for a time contemplated quitting football, contemplated dropping out of school. I had to go get professional help. And if it wasn't for one of my teammates who now actually plays in the NFL . . . pulling me to the side and stopping me from turning in my equipment, I would have quit football and dropped out of [name of university].

James's story about how this "tough day at the office" caused him to seek professional help and how one of his teammates persuaded him to go on is a powerful reminder of how matters at the individual and interpersonal levels can influence Black male athletes' educational experiences and outcomes.

James offered several recommendations to athletics administrators and other educational stakeholders to improve the relationship between college sport participation and educational outcomes for Black male college athletes. He tied his suggestions back to some thoughts he shared at the very beginning of our interview. James contended that there is a need to "redefine what education is." He was particularly concerned with "this gap of transferable skills and particularly marketable job skills, and being able to bring student-athletes in and interest and excite student-athletes through relevant and engaging content versus traditional education of getting a degree and have a resume and go to this internship and graduate on time of the standard education."

James's point was that instead of defining for these athletes what education should look like and how the educational process should unfold for them, athletic departments should "do a needs assessment asking your students what they want to get out of the college experience, because that's a gap right there in itself." As an entrepreneur and development professional, James often visited student development staff in Division I football and basketball programs at HWCU and engaged the professionals and the athletes in these programs in conversations about personal branding, exposing athletes to alternative means of income and career paths, and transitioning out of college sport, among other topics. He shared an example of a conversation he had with one athlete in one of these programs:

> I was on campus at [name of university] a couple weeks ago meeting with their student-athlete development staff . . . and a student-athlete came up to me. He asked . . . [what I did]. I said, "I'm an entrepreneur." He said "Wow, I want to be an entrepreneur!" And so we started talking. It turns out he loves shoes, so I was encouraging him to . . . understand consumer behavior on males eighteen to twenty-five who buy

shoes. And when you find that out, being able to provide those exact shoes they want in the exact place they want it. So having those kind of conversations . . . He could have a career out of that. But that will never show up on a degree program. So being willing to redefine what that looks like and not necessarily getting stuck in, "You have to do this degree to get this job," where, if you ask me, I have an undergraduate degree in exercise science, and what I'm doing right now has nothing to do with exercise science.

This is a great example of what James meant by redefining education and engaging athletes so that they begin to think more deeply about the possibilities for using their passions and interests to make a living and life for themselves after their college playing careers are over.

James's commentary prompted me to specifically engage him in a conversation on education scholar Gloria Ladson-Billings's idea of culturally relevant pedagogy—a student-centered approach to teaching where educators display cultural competence in relating to and using students' unique cultural strengths and backgrounds to help maximize their learning potential.[5] James discussed how his coaches were his best teachers during his time as a college athlete because they made concerted, genuine efforts to relate to him culturally:

[T]hey knew how to relate to me and they knew how to give me high-level content and break it down and use analogies that I understood. And every single team meeting we had, they played hip-hop music. Every single analogy we had, it had something to do with a relevant topic in our lives, of what was going on. They would use our language and not try to be cool, but just incorporate it into things that we experienced.

This is why James found it perplexing that "a football coach can teach an at-risk, low academic performing student-athlete high-level offensive or defensive concepts and get them to perform in front of hundreds of thousands of people at a high level" but these same athletes struggle mightily to do math in the classroom. James argued that "there's a gap in the delivery of information" in the university classroom and other educational settings. In his work on diversity, opportunity gaps, and teaching, Rich Milner discusses how in order to truly serve all students well, particularly racial and ethnic minority students, educators need to look at gaps in how they are teaching.[6] James's desire to "take that coaching mind-set into education" suggests he sees this as one effective approach to addressing the opportunity gaps in the education of Black male college athletes. It is an opportunity to connect with these athletes in a way that taps into their interests to bring out the best in them.

Finally, and related to this idea of opportunity gaps, James ended our interview with a discussion of how the attrition of Black male college athletes is a serious education matter that warrants more attention. He shared how "when I joined the [name of university] football team, there were twenty-five other football players who came in with me that year . . . Only five actually graduated." He further discussed how players might get kicked off the team, transfer, or go on medical hardship and "then nobody tracks them anymore. And that's just a guy who's lost in the system." In reflecting on his own experience with transferring, James was glad that he had the wherewithal to take care of himself so that he did not fall through the cracks and become that "'Where are they now,' VH1 type kid" from rapper Erick Sermon's quote in the introduction. James was particularly concerned about paying greater attention to what happens to Black male athletes in the window of time from when they first come to these HWCU and before their eligibility expires, and doing more to educate them during their time on campus. He concluded,

I think that's a huge problem that nobody's really talking about. Because the focus is either on graduation or career outcomes, but there's a whole lot more that don't make it even to graduation. And when they leave the college system, the support is immediately cut off.

WILLIS: FROM CAREER-ENDING INJURIES TO OPPORTUNITIES FOR ENGAGEMENT BEYOND THE GRIDIRON

I retired going into my true senior year. So my redshirt junior year . . . right before camp, but ended up staying on the team. I was like a student coach. That was the year we went to the Bowl game, which was a phenomenal experience. But I saw things from a zoomed-out angle and was able to kind of piece some things together just in terms of the coaches and where they go, what they do; the players, where they go, what they do; and just how peripheral academics was to athletics—which is the foundation, not the other way around. And you know, you get it while you're in it, but when you're out of it, you understand, like "OK, this is a real business."

Unlike the other Black male athletes interviewed for this chapter, Willis never got beyond his second year playing college sport. Due to sport-related knee, hip, and groin injuries he suffered beginning early in high school and into college and his doctor's advice to seriously consider giving up college football, Willis made the prudent decision to retire with two years of eligibility still remaining. Although this premature end to his playing career was disappointing, the decision allowed Willis to step back and really begin to see and better understand big-time college sport for what it really is: a massive commercial enterprise that operates very much like its professional sport counterpart. Perhaps most importantly, this end to his playing career also afforded him the opportunity to become more engaged in other developmentally useful activities outside of college sport competition. Willis's reflections about how the election of President Barack Obama in 2008 profoundly shaped his mind-set and perspective early on in his career as a young wide receiver at a major FBS program are particularly noteworthy:

> [I]t was big, like "Oh my God! We got a Black president!" . . . My family was just really happy, and like it just, it was a spout of joy and a feeling of, "I can do anything!" And it came at an opportune time because . . . I was starting, but it wasn't going very well, and then just having that and seeing that was like, "You know what? This is not the end all, be all . . . There's a lot more to life." So I started to get more involved in different areas. I started joining different clubs and doing stuff like that. I ended up pledging a fraternity, became president of the chapter and president of the national Panhellenic council on campus.

Willis's elaboration on his involvement in these leadership roles and other activities beyond college football provides important insight into why the transition out of football was not as difficult for him as it typically can be for so many other Black male college athletes:

> The connection with the fraternity, being, again, around a network of Black men who are achieving I think was highly beneficial to my thought process as I transitioned out of sports. A lot of folks get

depressed, but I think when I transitioned out, it was seamless . . . I still had that team aspect, and I still had the development aspect, and I had that leadership aspect . . . It was like, you know, when you leave the sport that you've done most of your life it's, like, "Oh my God." But it wasn't as bad . . . I remember I had a conversation with my dad about it, and he was like, "You know, we all have to do it at some point . . . but you're doing it right now when you still have a lot of support . . . Most folks, they do it and they're just in the world by themselves and have to go back to where they're from."

The support mechanisms and other identities that Willis established outside being a college football player were highly instrumental in helping him transition away from the gridiron and into the next phases of his life.

Prior to attending college and playing football at the HWCU where he earned both a bachelors and master's degree, Willis had fairly broad P–12 educational experiences. He went to an elementary school that was a "pretty diverse, international education school so we had a lot of different pieces to our curriculum," which gave him "a great foundation to deal with different folks and understand the politics of having friends of different races and stuff like that." The majority of his teachers were White, but Willis shared a powerful story about an older Black female teacher who "stood out a lot" and played a pivotal role in providing support for him when he was going through a difficult time as a third grader. Willis was going through a phase "where I didn't feel smart," especially when he was asked a question by the teacher and could not answer it. He revealed that after he went to the bathroom to cry one day, this Black female teacher sensed something was wrong and pulled him out in the hallway to talk. According to Willis, the teacher

> . . . was like, "What happened? Are you okay?" And I was like "I just don't feel smart, I don't feel smart." And I remember she quickly was like, "Never say that again . . . You are smart, you are intelligent, and anybody who can't see different doesn't know the real definition of being smart." . . . I was like "Man, this is crazy. My teacher really can see this in me." You know, you can tell the difference when somebody's inauthentic and when somebody is actually talking to your soul. And I believe at that point she was talking to my soul.

Willis was fascinated by this teacher's willingness to extend to him the support and love that was constantly reinforced and given to him at home. These empowering interactions set a strong foundation for Willis going forward.

Willis attended middle schools that had more Black and Brown students than his elementary school, and he was considered one of the "cool kids" who earned mostly A's. In reflecting on his time in middle school, Willis stated "I was considered really smart in a lot of my classes, did really good work, but I had my challenges." In particular, math was one of the subjects he was "great at," but he "hated [science] dearly." It was his Black male science teacher who helped him see science in a different way:

> [H]e helped me see . . . the fun part about learning it, not just the schooling part, where you have to learn this for the test and you have to do this to go to the next grade . . . But he helped me see that . . . the fundamental piece of [science] is problem solving . . . We're looking for ways to help people when they're sick, to help people push forward in terms of how to put different elements together to create things, stuff like that. So I mean, I saw a practical piece of using science versus let me just learn this for the next grade.

This science teacher helped Willis begin to see science as something he could identify with and use as a practical tool to develop self and help others. Instead of following the formal schooling process that involved training him to acquiesce to White hegemonic norms and linear ways of thinking and doing, he was more interested in the true education that occurs when students of color are exposed to relevant ideas that allow them to better understand themselves and their relationship to the subject matter, and extend it beyond the classroom setting.[7]

Willis related another interesting experience during middle school where his language arts teacher, a Latinx female, encouraged him to break away from the constraints that the schooling process can often place on students' creativity:

> So we're writing a paper, and . . . she was teaching us the five-paragraph model; you know, conclusion, three body paragraphs, stuff like that . . . and I'm like "[Name of teacher], why do we do this? Why can't

we just write in any kind of free style?" And she was like, "You know what, you can. Why don't you change it? You write the way you want to write it and I'll look at it and judge it accordingly." I'm like, "OK, I didn't expect you to say that. I expected you to be like 'Why are you questioning?'" But she was like, "You go ahead and be different . . . and I want you to write how you want to write."

Willis had fond memories of these experiences with his teachers because they seemed more invested in his education, not merely just confining him to the schooling process. It is also worth noting that middle school is when Willis became formally involved in playing football and basketball, and he was fortunate to have his father and uncles coach and help nurture his development in this learning context outside the classroom.

At his father's suggestion, Willis ended up attending a predominantly White all-boys private high school. Initially, he was very reluctant to attend this school, which was not so culturally diverse. He eventually agreed because both his parents helped him understand that the high school you choose to attend "is going to really springboard you into what college you get into, not just academically but athletically as well." The fact that this private school "had . . . between probably 99, 100 percent graduation rate, and then college acceptance about 95 percent" was a strong selling point for Willis. Moreover, his father's promise to continue coaching him convinced Willis to stay. His father ended up being his ninth-grade position coach at the school, and continued to be instrumental in helping Willis develop into a college football prospect and support him through his myriad injuries and other challenges in high school. For example, his father got up early every morning and did rehabilitation exercises with Willis when he was recovering from one of the injuries he suffered playing football.

Willis was one of only four Black males on the football team at this private school, and only one of "about ten Black people" in a majority-White school of "about close to nine hundred kids." He shared with me how he struggled in the required theology class at this "Jesuit school," particularly "trying to learn Catholicism, and from a White lens," especially the images of a "blond and blue-eyed Jesus everywhere." The image was troublesome for him and his Black teammates because it did not represent the image of Jesus they knew. Fortunately, Willis was able to lean on various supports, including a male Indian educator who asked Willis one day if he was okay and said to him, "[T]his is a White environment . . . what they think and what you know are two different things." This educator let Willis know the door of his office was always open if he ever needed support in navigating that environment. Similar to the Black students Beverly Tatum discussed in her book *Why Are All the Black Kids Sitting Together in the Cafeteria?* Willis and his Black teammates relied heavily on the multicultural services office in the school as a daily "safe space" to congregate with peers and people who looked like them during breaks and lunchtime.[8] Even though "the administration tried to break it up" and make them "go somewhere else," Willis shared how that lived experience of congregating in that office space every day allowed his Black peers and him to nurture themselves as cultural beings and make "fun of our experiences." However, they also understood that they were "in a unique position to be at a school that was academically prestigious and kind of go through that rigorous academic training." This would become evident to Willis after he accepted an athletic scholarship to play football in an FBS program at a HWCU. He also enrolled in the college's summer bridge academic program to help athletes transition into higher education. Willis began to see "how much better my schooling was than a lot of my classmates" in the bridge program.

Willis had a major breakthrough season during his junior year in high school and attended multiple football camps the summer after. He attracted interest from several Division I schools, including an Ivy League school that offered him a grant and aid. But he "felt intimidated" by the school, and opted instead to accept an athletic scholarship to play football at a major FBS conference school that had a strong academic and athletics reputation. As mentioned at the outset of this vignette, Willis's playing career ended prematurely due to injuries. Nonetheless, his participation in college sport provided some great educational experiences and opportunities. In particular, the head football coach during his first two years was one of the very few Black males to be a head coach for the roughly 120 NCAA Division I football programs at the time. (Many scholars, as well as the Black male athletes I featured in chapter 2, have discussed how the presence of Black athletics leaders at HWCU is critically important to the education of Black male athletes.) Willis related how this coach made it a priority to expose the young men he coached to influential and powerful Black people outside the university:

I'd never met with so many Black folks that were influential in the com-
munity in my life. Like he had the Breakfast Club come speak to us
. . . He had like really big figureheads in [name of city], like powerful
Black folks come and have lunch with us during camp.

This head coach was a clean-cut role model who "didn't cuss . . . didn't
drink . . . and didn't smoke weed" and always respectfully addressed the
athletes he coached as men. Moreover, Willis shared how this coach would
have frank conversations with the Black male athletes on his team about
about the realities outside of school:

> [I]n private conversations with the Black men, he said, "This world's
> not built for you." But he said, "You have to succeed in it." He said,
> "Football is going to end. But you're going to have to be a man for the
> rest of your life . . . so you have to figure out what that means for you,
> and move forward into life with that understanding and continue to
> develop what you're building here."

Willis admitted that he did not quite value or fully appreciate what his coach
was doing for him at the time. Now he realizes this coach "was beyond his
time and was doing stuff then that folks are now trying to institute" in
terms of "getting us in front of people, helping us develop ourselves, and
helping us look at ourselves in a different light."

Unfortunately, given the heavy focus on winning and commercial
development in college sport, this coach was fired after a couple of unsuc-
cessful seasons. Willis finished out the remainder of his abbreviated playing career under another head coach who had more success in the win-loss
column.

Although Willis wrestled with getting his priorities in order during his first year in the program and initially struggled academically—
interestingly enough, in math, a subject he did well with in P–12—he
eventually got on the right path. By the time he retired from college football, he had begun to gain a firm understanding of the "hidden curriculum"
in the US educational system and "how to be politically mobile and deal
with White folks." This, to him, was more akin to being truly educated,
although he did acknowledge the importance of getting the academic "nuts
and bolts of school." Willis took the mind-set of being civically engaged,

being politically mobile, being able to communicate with different types of people, and being able to exist in the world and express his identity and learn other peoples' identities into his master's program and eventually into his doctoral studies. When I interviewed him, he had recently completed his doctoral studies and plans to use his formal schooling and education to create influence and opportunities with and for the students and others he works with as a leader in higher education and beyond.

When asked how his participation in big-time college sport contributed to this ongoing process of education, Willis exclaimed, "It made me visible! It made me visible!" This visibility on campus encouraged Willis to seek out "how people saw me and how I saw myself" in that learning environment. This helped him learn how to successfully code-switch "to get to where you want and need to be" in life. Willis gave major credit to the academic athletic support staff—particularly an older Black woman who was a "longtime legend" and "the backbone of a lot of training and development that happened for Black athletes" at the university—with helping him to navigate and negotiate the sometimes difficult educational terrain of this HWCU.

As we concluded our conversation, Willis offered some blunt recommendations for the people who oversee and manage college sport. In particular, his critique focused on the often incompatible goals and priorities of commercial versus human development in this age of academic capitalism. First and foremost, he asserted that decision makers need to "stop treating us like dollars" and only as "spectacles to be witnessed." Willis expressed disdain for how these stakeholders of college sport often try to "take away the humanness of us because we pay bills in certain areas." He explicitly suggested that leaders across these campuses need to "stop making education auxiliary" to the athletics enterprise and make more concerted efforts to better integrate athletics into the broader campus environment. He also emphasized that HWCU need to stop isolating Black male football and basketball athletes and some of their peers from other learning opportunities outside the athletics department. He likened this practice to "intellectually incarcerating" them and taking "away a lot of possibilities for their future." Scholars, other social commentators, and reform-minded groups and individuals have discussed this idea for decades, and some of my more recent research has shown that there are at least a few examples of athletic departments that are integrating athletics into the broader university environment.[9]

Finally, Willis conveyed that it is very important for the educational stakeholders who work with Black male athletes on HWCU campuses to "stop treating us like we're stupid" and acknowledge that "it takes a lot of intelligence to play sports, especially football" at the college level. He cautioned that "when you continually treat them as if they're stupid, they embody that." Willis suggested these stakeholders must acknowledge the intelligence and ability of Black male athletes to process and "make kinaesthetic decisions in split seconds" during sport competition, and leverage that to help them transfer this greatness to life outside college sport.

MARC: BALANCING TENURED FACULTY AND ATHLETICS ADMINISTRATOR ROLES

What's on my mind is trying to, in my work now, work with athletes and work with the system in which the athletes are a part of. I don't see myself only working with athletes. I also see myself working with the system that athletes are a part of—so that system meaning with [athletic] administrators and with the coaches, with the academic support, with the faculty and the university administration, working with the surrounding community. So that's fans, including the various levels of donors. All of these stakeholders, combined with the culture of sport within society, constitute much of what is the system in which the education for athletes is supposed to be happening. All of this is part of the kind of pedagogical structure, which educates them or miseducates them. So that's what I'm thinking about in my work now. To some degree, my approach to this work can look slightly different based on who the stakeholder is at the moment.

And . . . this sounds really like a jigsaw puzzle, but I'm thinking about this is the target and this is the moment now, but it has to connect to last week's moment and it has to connect to possibly next week's moment with something else. So I'm always trying to put that jigsaw puzzle together on, What is the type of education that I'm really after for these students? And that shifts . . . with the times, the climate of the day and the era. It shifts with the type of athlete that comes in one year after another. It shifts with the cohort they come in with. It has shifted with the change of head coaches and change of administration . . . I work with. When it begins to feel as if we were on target and . . . [all of a sudden] . . . the goalposts shift a little bit. And so, how do you adjust in that moment, where you've always got the same goal but the pathway, you know, you've got to be nimble in the system . . . that's what I mean by working with the athletes.

Similar to the other former Black male college athletes I interviewed for this chapter, I began the conversation by inviting Marc to offer any thoughts related to Black male athlete education matters that might have been foremost in his mind. Marc's insightful response above can be better understood and appreciated when you consider the two different hats he wears as a thirty-four-year-old senior-level athletics administrator and tenured faculty member at the Division I HWCU where he played college football. Managing the demands of these two roles places Marc in a unique position to navigate and address the sometimes competing interests and priorities of various stakeholder groups of this athletic department and university. Moreover, Marc's status as a former standout offensive lineman at this HWCU who had a brief stint in the NFL, and his background as a scholar who has published work related to race, sport, and education makes his story and perspective on Black male athlete education matters all the more fascinating.

Marc is the oldest child of Black, African immigrant father and a White mother who was born and raised in a large Southwestern city. Early in our conversation, he shared the difference in how his parents viewed education, and the impact it had on him:

> So they have two different paths when it comes to their formal education. School seemed to turn her off, and education ignited my father, which is kind of interesting on how these two mix. I've always had a really strong view of the power of what education could possibly do for someone, influenced by my father's . . . thirst for an education.

Although he briefly attended college but never finished, Marc's father really stressed how education was the "next step" and "ticket in life"—a necessary "stamp on the passport to get to where you need to be" and "move up the . . . socioeconomic ladder." As a result, Marc developed this "sense of my education was to not let my father down. My father had tried and persevered, that for me to not do well in school would be to let him down." Marc felt it was "on me to carry the torch wherever he left off." Marc's mother "grew up . . . lower-middle class, working class," and often talked about "how much she didn't like school" (by ninth grade, she had dropped out of school). In fact, Marc shared how his mother being "turned off" by school made it difficult for her to be engaged with him during his early schooling. Marc recalls how she wanted him to do well, but "her sense of incompetency to support that limited her ability" to help him in school. Nevertheless, she encouraged him to "go beyond your father in terms of education."

Marc's father had been a cab driver but became a truck driver when Marc was in elementary school, and this required him to be away for long periods. Marc discussed how only seeing his father a few months at a time during those formative school years impacted his education. He was unable to read until the third grade, but was still just pushed from one grade to the next. When his father found out, things began to change:

> [My] father came home from one of his truck-driving trips and real-ized that I couldn't read. I sat on . . . a broken Lazy Boy chair we had, and I was reading to him and I couldn't finish the sentence . . . I was able to read some words like "I" and "in" but I couldn't put full sen-tences together. So it set him off . . . he immediately picked up another job . . . so he worked two jobs. I never saw him, but he . . . sent me to a private school not too far away. I had to go to the early childhood day care at this school, because it was way out of my neighborhood. I would get dropped off about 5:00 in the morning. And then my mother would pick me up on her way home. So I did that for about three-quarters of a year because we could only pay for that much. I remember that the bills were coming in and eventually we were just too far behind. So I essentially got kicked out of the school, and they took me back to my school, the elementary I was at.

However, the short time he spent at the private school was beneficial. According to Marc, "When I came back to my elementary late into the third-grade year, [all of a sudden], I went from being fairly illiterate at the back of my class to number-two, number-three in that class."

Marc reflected on how it "sat with me" that it took him leaving his neighborhood "to do well in school." Being back in the public school helped Marc realize that the education he was receiving "wasn't good enough," and that he longed for greater preparation. He "knew that something about this elementary school, something about being in this neighborhood meant that we didn't get the same type of education that they got on the other side of town." Marc became aware of the disparities in resources between the private school and the neighborhood elementary school he was forced to go back to. He also knew that he was a smart and competitive student who had an "ego about me at a very young age," and that "some of my pushback, a kind of dissent and resistance in the classroom, wasn't so much that I was a bad kid, it was just I didn't trust what I was being fed in that school." Perhaps this explains in part why, as he approached middle school, Marc and his mother were receptive to the idea of him enrolling in a free summer program designed to prepare students to be different from everyone else in school. He gave an interesting example of discussions about the O. J. Simpson trial to demonstrate how students in this program were getting a "different type of education" than the other students in the school:

> I was introduced to O. J. Simpson in [that] class. And we had different kinds of conversations because of the cohort that I was in when that moment happened . . . The teacher had her racist comment . . . "That man got away." At the same time, she also said, "Well, let's talk about . . . what's happening in the world right now." No other kid in that school was learning about O. J. Simpson and what was happening in the world at that time . . . [We were], even if it was coming from a teacher who we recognized had certain racist views about the trial . . .

In reflecting on that time, Marc realized that education involved more than just learning about basic subject matter in the curriculum; it extended to students being exposed to important matters in the broader society. The conversations about contemporary issues beyond the basic curriculum that he was partaking in during the summer program represented that "different type of education" from peers who were not in the program.

The only sport Marc played growing up was soccer because his family could not afford the equipment that was required for him to play sports such as football. He began playing football in eighth grade, when he also played basketball. Once his junior high football coaches saw that he was a "big kid" who "was pretty strong" they "pushed me into the weight room quite a bit." By the end of his freshman year in high school Marc was moved up to the varsity football team, where he became a key player from his sophomore year on. Although he played for a large high school in a tradition-rich state known for consistently producing Division I talent, his team won only two games, both in his senior year, in the three years he played varsity. Despite the team's lack of success, Marc demonstrated potential to play Division I college football; and that potential became more pronounced his senior year, when a new head coach pushed him to believe he could play college football. For the first time, Marc realized his potential and began to understand the process involved for getting to college.

Marc graduated from high school with roughly a 3.8 grade point average and was recruited by schools in major FBS conferences. He ended up accepting an athletic scholarship to play football in the Division I program mentioned earlier. Part of the reason Marc chose this school was because it provided him a "fresh start" and an "independence" or way to "forge my own path." He also appreciated that the head coach "gave me a good vibe" and was interested in building his program around the recruitment and development of "character guys" like him. Marc believed this coach "saw something in me in a kind of positive quality of character that I appreciated, and I was on board with that. And then I got there, met the guys, and I thought I could play there."

When asked how his participation in college sport influenced his education, Marc's first response was to share how from day one, the academic expectations for players in his cohort were lowered by academic counselors in the athletic department:

> I show up to [name of school], the first year the academic director . . . brings a few of us rookies in. We were all Black and one White guy, I think about seven of us. He pulled us [into] his office and he hands us our schedule . . . and on my schedule, I had a military skills class where we would look at maps. I did first aid, which . . . probably takes nowadays three days to complete; it took us a semester. It was about trying to boost your GPA, and that literally was what he said: "We're going to get a good start, you all are going to kind of feel out the ropes this first semester. Most of you won't play." And most of us didn't play. He said, "You won't play but you're going to practice. The transition's going to be hard so we want you to kind of get a good start."

Marc said that, on the surface, what this academic director was saying seemed logical to him as an eighteen-year-old freshman. However, reflecting on the fact that he was a good student coming into the university, he realized that "the expectation was . . . lowered . . . that very moment" that academic director handed him his schedule. The message that was sent and received was that they were there to first and foremost play football. Some of my previous formal and informal research as well as a review of the extant literature, including the work of Eddie Comeaux, suggests that the lowering of academic expectations for Black male athletes in football and basketball programs at HWCU is commonplace.

In further critically reflecting on his educational experiences, Marc constantly stated how the educational process for his teammates and him was this "prescribed . . . system of efficiency" designed to push athletes through from first year to graduation. The system was not designed to challenge them to be "curious about who you are, where you are, where you're going, what you're doing, and why you're doing it." From Marc's perspective, education by definition is that thing or process which should bring out a certain level of consciousness and curiosity in students, and that the system of efficiency that most Black male athletes are subjected to at these HWCU too often takes away this "kind of power of curiosity" that is so critical to their growth and development in college and beyond. He stated that when he thinks back to his time as a college athlete, it sometimes "angers me about what I could have done. I always think back about what else I would have majored in had I known what I know now." Marc had expressed an interest in studying business and actually visited the business school during the recruitment process. But once on campus, he was discouraged from pursuit of that degree and never set foot in the business school building again. He ended up graduating with a degree in health and exercise science.

Marc expressed how his educational experiences as a college athlete greatly influenced "the types of programming we put on for athletes" in his role as a senior-level athletics administrator:

> I'm trying to expose them in ways that the system is not built to do. The system is built to be efficient . . . The system's not built to really expose our athletes to the nuances and the opportunities, the resources of a land grant institution built around agriculture . . . I know that many of my athletes don't come from that background . . . at least the ones who share my shade of skin.

Marc was interested in using his position as an athletics administrator and faculty member at the university to disrupt the system of efficiency that too often fails to provide Black male college athletes with a "curious education." One of his goals was to get athletes to that place where they are asking critical questions such as "What does it mean to be a leader when you're in Flint, Michigan, and the water's been tainted? [How] do you lead a community back to a place where they can thrive and feel safe?" Marc acknowledged the important role this system of education plays in helping Black male college athletes to obtain "certain skills" and "build your toolkit," but from his perspective,

> an education without making someone curious, an education without giving people the ability of how to ask questions and when to ask questions and to interrogate, to apply really hard content to very ambiguous problems, how do you connect these two worlds? If we're not doing that, then we're not truly educating them. We're not educating them, we're just graduating.

Marc posed powerful rhetorical questions: "How easy is it to get everybody across the stage with a 2.0? . . . How hard is it to get across the stage with how to use a 2.0 to change the world?" These words drive home the point that if these HWCU only focus on graduating Black male athletes but not educating them during their time on campus, they have done them a great disservice.

In acknowledging that he is an educational stakeholder in college sport who works with both the athletes and the system, Marc borrowed a metaphor he had once heard a Christian preacher from back home use: "We can't just worry about how to nurture the seed, we got to fix the soil, right?" He further elaborated, "So it's the soil of the institution, it's the soil of a college athletic department. The culture in which the seed is growing, where the athletes are growing, maturing." Similar to what I asserted in the introductory chapter of this book, Marc was keenly aware that we must first and foremost be concerned with what is "wrong" with the system instead of focusing primarily on what is supposedly "wrong" with the athlete and trying to "fix" the athlete instead of first addressing the system. In Marc's words,

That's the part of the problem that allows the system to keep working as is. That's what I'm working on, trying to figure that out. Yeah, we need mentoring, and yeah, we need programming, but that isn't to fix them. Like, you brought them in, now I have to come in and fix them. No, the soil's got to get fixed. So the policies and the practices, the culture, all of those are a part of this complex problem. I'm working to crack that.

Marc suggested that "the market that college athletics is and creates" is a macro- and meso-level matter and major component of the system that needs to be addressed in order for Black male athletes and their peers to be better served in the educational setting and culture of college sport. He was critical about how the "market" dictates decisions such as the exorbitant amount of money head football and basketball coaches are paid and how much power and influence these coaches are given over athletes and the athletic department more generally. Marc lamented this "coach as savior" mentality that permeates these HWCU, and insisted this mentality is dangerous to Black male athletes' education because it too often compels these athletes to capitulate to the market-driven agenda of these coaches, which could stifle their curiosity as students and athletes. In a 2018 article, Joy Gaston Gayles and her colleagues discuss how "neoliberal practices certainly send the message that student interests are less a priority than market interests, and individuals are to blame for their social positions, rather than the market or power structures."[10] Like Marc, these scholars argue that the market logics that drive the decisions of athletics stakeholders not only threaten the viability and sustainability of the system, but they also undermine opportunities for Black male athletes (and their peers) to maximize their potential beyond athletics participation.

In offering recommendations on how we might strengthen the college sport and education nexus to the benefit of Black male athletes and their peers, Marc was particularly concerned about the perspectives and approaches of the educational stakeholders who are on the front lines working directly with these athletes. He wondered to what extent these educational stakeholders' mind-sets and decision-making align with the needs of the athletes they serve. Marc offered the following observation about coaches as an example of a way to hold these powerful and influential educational stakeholders accountable:

I'd love to challenge a coach to . . . write themselves a contract of what they say on a recruiting spiel—what they're saying to parents and to the players. Write that down as if you were writing yourself a contract. And then to evaluate . . . or better yet, maybe have someone else or have your players evaluate where you have met the claim and where you're missing or if you're even facing the right direction. Write to yourself a definition of education and then to see how you actually met that, even if it might be a trivial idea of education. I'm just curious—How do you even think about it? How do you think about it and how do you meet that? From there, we could talk about where your own beliefs and standards could evolve to.

JAMES T.: LEADER BOTH ON AND OFF THE GRIDIRON AND HARDWOOD

So, as I aspire to be an athletics director in the future, two things that kind of stick out to me [we have the responsibility for]. And I speak more to the minority side because that's . . . where I resonate to, is that you've got to provide those student-athletes . . . the access and the opportunity. And by access, that's access to the proper training, proper resources. It could be academically, it could be educationally, athletically, emotionally, socially. Are we providing the access to the resources that they need to further their dream? And then the opportunity . . . are we providing these kids the proper opportunity for them to grow? Either in their sport, academically, in their professional career, opportunity is important. A lot of these kids are very talented, but they don't have the opportunity to show that talent. The opportunity to get in front of people. So that's kind of . . . my beacon as I grow within athletic administration, and . . . as I aspire to be an athletic director, to be able to impact student-athletes . . . How are we manufacturing opportunities for them to grow and learn? And that's . . . the conversations that I have amongst my colleagues and the people that I work with, and also the student-athletes.

At the time I interviewed him, James was an athletics administrator at a major FBS-affiliated university. The quote above was his response to my invitation for him to share his initial thoughts on the topic of Black male athlete education matters. I asked him to elaborate on what he meant by "proper" when referring to the training, resources, and opportunities that are necessary for Black male athletes to grow at HWCU. James acknowledged the value of these Division I athletic departments in providing athletes with access to certain training, resources, and opportunities, but asserted they should also align with what athletes deem to be valuable and appropriate for their growth and development. He insisted a gap exists because leaders and other educational stakeholders in athletic departments are not taking the time to really sit down with these athletes and discuss their goals, objectives, wants, and needs outside of sport. As an athletics administrator, James believed that providing proper opportunities for college athletes boils down to leaders in these programs giving athletes a seat at the table "to articulate what's important to them." I shared with James that inviting college athletes to literally sit at the table and share their experiences and thoughts with us during our monthly meetings is something I advocated and practiced during my time as the chair of the president's athletics council at Texas A&M University. To James' point, I found this to be the "proper" and right thing to do if we as educational stakeholders both within and outside the athletic department are genuinely concerned about their education and empowerment.

James was a standout athlete who played both football and basketball at a Division I mid-major HWCU. Given his unique role as a dual-sport athlete in the top two revenue-producing sports at the Division I level, I was particularly interested in learning if he felt that he was provided with proper opportunities on campus and as a team captain on both the gridiron and hardwood. James discussed the intense physical, mental, and time demands associated with balancing his participation in these two sports, which have overlapping seasons:

> It's very difficult. It's taxing mentally; it's taxing physically. I had to . . . change my body twice a year. I had to drop twelve pounds to play basketball, and then I would have to gain that weight back to play football. And that's wear and tear on your body. And mentally . . . you had to prioritize. I learned that at a really young age to prioritize my time, and I cannot waste time . . . And also I had to eliminate things in my life that wasn't in alignment with my goals.

James largely credited his ability to juggle these demands to his parents "instilling the importance of education" and certain values, habits, and discipline in him from a very young age. This was particularly the case with his father, who had "real man-to-man conversations" with James when he was growing up. He taught James to document and evaluate his goals in life and hold himself accountable for reaching them. The strong influence of his parents as well as "the people that I respected and my mentors" set him on the right path to having "an unbelievable collegiate experience." James related that he took "ownership of that experience in school and telling them what I wanted to get accomplished, what my goals are. And I think that, that helps for you to steward that experience." Unlike most of his teammates across both sports, James "never had aspirations to play professionally," so this helped him put things in perspective and really focus on his goals of getting a well-rounded college experience and earning his degree while he played "two sports that I loved dearly."

James recognized that the institution he played at did not have the abundant resources in terms of operating budgets and number of coaches and support staff, compared with FBS schools such as the one at which he was an athletics administrator. However, he still "maximized all of the opportunities that were afforded to me academically, you know, getting involved outside of my athletic responsibilities, getting involved with organizations on campus." James also shared how the athletic director at his alma mater, a Black male who was a former Division I football standout in college, played a pivotal role in his "unbelievable collegiate experience" and aspirations to one day become an athletic director himself:

> I think it was profound, and . . . I think it's important because when you're a young male, a young African American in this environment, it's a blessing to have . . . people that look like you in roles. And I think that's important because it's encouraging . . . even going back to a young James at that particular time in my life . . . I think it made me feel more comfortable to approach him. And think about it, you're a student-athlete and you have the ability to walk into the athletic director's office and ask him a question. That was his policy.

James further stated that this athletic director "is the reason why I have an aspiration to become an athletic director, because he had such a profound impact on my life as a student-athlete." James stressed how important it was for Black and Brown athletes at these HWCU to "see people who look like them" in influential positions beyond just professional athletes and coaches. Therefore, it was James' goal as an athletics administrator and future athletic director to be that mentor and example for the present and future generation of Black athletes. Research my colleague and I have conducted on the diversity best practices of Black male athletic directors at Division I HWCU speaks to the points James raised above.[11]

James's reflections about how he defines and conceptualizes education led to some interesting discourse. One of the constant themes to emerge was that education is a "tool for you to use, to better yourself" and to "learn about yourself, learn about other things, gain experiences. According to James,

> I look at it kind of in that form of a tool. How I look at education is that it's power as well . . . and when you're educated, you have this power. You're able to influence things. You're able to better yourself with education. You even have some type of mechanism of power. So I look at it as a tool, and then you have this bucket of power, of leverage or an asset, I would say. Maybe not power—*power* is probably not a good word. But an asset, something that you have. Something tangible or intangible . . . education, for me should be an experience too . . . I have learned, I've gained so many experiences through education. And that could just be me going to a retreat with a number of student-athletes from all over the world and through education, I was able to gather all of these awesome experiences.

In response to these ideas and his questioning whether *power* was the right word to use to describe what education does for Black male athletes, I discussed historian John Henrik Clarke's conceptualization of education for Black people (discussed in chapter 1). Clarke describes education as a process of understanding the power one has and properly using it to effectuate change to one's conditions. I also shared with James the example of the University of Missouri football players' use of their collective power and influence as a tool to bring about policy and personnel changes on campus. This example prompted James to exclaim, "That's what I said too, and I'm happy you kind of reaffirmed it, is that the education piece is power and then they figured out how to use that as a tool for change."

In our discussions about the particular role college sport played in contributing to his education, James came back to this idea of access and opportunity:

So football and basketball afforded me the opportunity to . . . select the institution that best aligns with what I wanted to do. I wanted to go to college . . . I wanted to be a college football quarterback at a school that was close to home. That was my goal—bam, bam, bam . . . I wouldn't have had the opportunity—again, I'm speculating, I can't go back and rewrite history—But for me personally . . . if I didn't excel in sports, I don't think I would have had the opportunity to be that specific in what I wanted to do.

Although James was a good student in high school (above a 3.0 GPA) who was recruited by several schools, including Ivy League schools, around the nation for both football and basketball, his mother's passing during this time changed his perspective, and thus his recruitment process. He wanted to stay close to home and have an opportunity to play quarterback for a Division I football program with the option to play basketball. The mid-major institution where he ended up accepting an athletic scholarship aligned well with James' needs and objectives at that crucial point in his life. James' college sport participation journey is a great example of that "proper opportunity" to learn and grow that he articulated in the quote at the outset of this narrative.

In offering final thoughts and recommendations for improving the nexus of college sport participation and positive educational outcomes for Black male college athletes, James shared "where the gaps are." In particular, he discussed the divide we sometimes see between college sport leaders and college athletes who "are quote-unquote millennials." As a thirty-two-year-old who is "kind of on the fringe of" this generation, James suggested this generation of college athletes want to know why they are being asked to do something, and how doing it could benefit them both on and off the field or court. While offering the caveat that one should not put all millennials in a box or lump them together, James did provide this general assessment of this generation of college athletes:

Millennials want to ask the question, "Why?" They don't take direction very well. Like, "Dr. Singer, do X, Y and Z. This is what you got to do." The question that they typically ask is, "You got to explain it to me how this is going to benefit me. Explain how, why I'm doing this. What's the byproduct? Give me the background." They want data and information to justify actions. And I don't think there's nothing wrong with that. Conversely, from an older perspective, a lot of these older individuals grew up on, "You tell me what to do, and I'll do it." Questioning or inquiring why is perceived as defiance and that's not a good thing, where I think it's the opposite of that. [Millenials are] invested, they want to know more, and the more information you give them, the more invested they will be, the more they're going to align with it and run through a brick wall for you.

James believed there are notable gaps "between the athletics piece and the educational piece," and that college sport leaders and administrators should do better at articulating how the process of education and being a college student can help them athletically and how participating in athletics can help them educationally. James suggested that college sport leaders should utilize the "many educational examples within college sports" to help college athletes better understand the nexus of sport participation and their education. He reflected on college sport strength and conditioning programs and his own experiences as a college athlete to convey this idea:

[E]ven from like a strength and condition perspective—like our strength and condition staff I know they're the best in the country, they're awesome at what they do. It's because they really sit down with the student-athletes and educate them on the importance of being in the weight room. When I was a student-athlete, I hated the weight room, it sucked. It was a punishment because they didn't explain to me why I'm lifting this weight. Why are you lifting this amount of weight? Why are you coming in when you're sore? How you can recover. And understanding, "OK, if you do this, James, you're going to be a better athlete, and by being a better athlete, that's going to make you a better football player. By being a better football player, that's going to get you to the next level." So now I'm educated, they walked me through the process, now I'm attacking that weight room experience in a different way because I'm educated. And that's where I see, in terms of the student athletes that I work with, is that "Why am I running all these sprints?" . . . It really comes to the *why*, and the *why* isn't from a defiant place. The *why* is a cry-out saying, "Educate me, tell me why, break this down for me." And that's the gap, that's what I see. Maybe

I'm blinded, but that's where I can see the connection between college sports and education, and that's the gap.

To make sure I understood his point, I asked if he thought the education of Black male athletes goes beyond the coursework, the GPA, graduation, and all those measures we typically use to define whether or not somebody is achieving in the world of education. James responded, "Yeah, that's a profound way of looking at it." James was critical of this status quo approach to assessing the education of college athletes, asserting that it is "very cookie-cutter, and if you don't check these boxes, you fail academically." But he did acknowledge

> there has to be some baseline understanding, I get that piece . . . our education has to have some curriculum behind it. But also, as educators, we got to be dynamic as well, and cater to the need of that student in developing curriculum that's beneficial to them from an education piece. I know that's heavy and that's gonna be like turning the ship, it's going to take some time, but I think that's an opportunity for us to grow in that area . . . I don't fancy to say that I have the answers . . . my goal is "Let's create some dialogue around those challenges in hopes that we have a cohort of people that will help create a solution." And I would love to be a part of that cohort.

ARCHIE: FINDING PURPOSE AND FILLING GAPS AFTER ATHLETIC COMPETITION

I would love to see more tools in place, more systems in place to support our athletes in particular, but potentially our Black male athletes as far as not only while they're here, but even more so as they transition out . . . and making sure that they are prepared to be able to start their own business or to be able to work for someone else so that they can be fully employed and be able to provide for their families as they leave these institutions.

Archie's opening quote speaks to the importance he places on preparing Black male athletes for their eventual transition out of big-time college sport participation and retirement from elite-level sport more generally. Like so many other talented Black male football and basketball athletes who come through these programs, this thirty-something-year-old former wide receiver turned defensive back in a HWCU tradition-rich Division I football program aspired to transition from college sport into a successful career as a professional athlete. And he seemed to be well on his way to doing just that after a sophomore year in which he was one of the leaders in the nation in interceptions as a cornerback with the great size—he stands over six feet tall—and athleticism that NFL scouts covet. But in the summer after his breakout season, a car accident changed his fate. Due to the injuries he sustained, Archie no longer possessed the athletic prowess that had helped land him his athletic scholarship and starting role on the football team.

Archie battled back from his injuries to regain a starting cornerback position his senior year. But he admitted how tough it was to go from being a star cornerback to seeing one of his backups step in and go on to become a successful NFL player—something he probably would have done had it not been for his injuries. Archie also struggled with the reality that people began to treat him differently "when I stopped playing and I wasn't out there making interceptions . . . people wouldn't return my [calls] as much, or they weren't calling at all." Archie detailed his struggles dealing with his new reality and making that transition out of playing elite-level football:

> I was borderline depressed, especially after my senior year, when people I played against, people I knew who were getting drafted and pursuing their dream, and I'm trying to get a job at a rental car company. And then trying to see if someone in the CFL [Canadian Football League] would give me an opportunity or this, that, and the other . . . I was definitely bitter and depressed. I didn't watch football for a long time . . . it was [a] tough transition, because I identified so much with being the athlete. And now I knew that no longer was the case.

Like so many other Black male college athletes (e.g., Bobby from chapter 2), Archie had to grapple with the sobering reality of transitioning away from his athlete identity to other salient identities.[12] As will be discussed in more detail below, Archie's transitioning out of elite-level sport participation (what he describes as an "eye-opening experience about life"), along with other major life events, including divorce, that happened years later, prompted him to found and establish a nonprofit organization to help former athletes find their purpose and fill the gaps in their life after their playing days have ended.

In reflecting back on that challenging time when his injuries essentially forced him to shift gears and pursue other life goals beyond professional sport, Archie shared how thankful he was that "I had my family, who stressed the importance of education. And I had some other skill sets, but if I didn't, who knows where I would have ended up?" Archie discussed how the strong expectations his grandfather, father, and mother placed on him to pursue education—which he viewed at the time as simply a process that allows a person "to be informed on whatever the topic might be"—definitely played an important role in helping him navigate the difficult times he faced during his college playing days. He also discussed how his strong Christian faith, which was greatly influenced by his mother being an evangelist and his father a pastor, "played a huge, huge role" in helping him mentally get "through some of the downtime" when he was in college. In fact, Archie became affectionately known as "the good rev" among his college teammates and would actually "get the guys together on Sundays" to go to church. He also "was the one doing the prayer or . . . was the one empowered by the coaches to decide who's doing the prayer" and became "like the go-to guy when it came to the spiritual aspect on our team."

When asked to share how his participation in college sport helped contribute to his education, Archie provided multiple examples. First, he mentioned "the amount of structure—structure and time management." He discussed how the structure that college sport gave him as an athlete helped him with "the time management and also to be able to prioritize." He further elaborated on this point:

> [W]ith sports, sometimes you got to make calculated decisions of which play do you want to run or which pass you're going to make or which route you're going to cut off. So be able to translate that to education as far as we have this agenda or this syllabus, so prioritizing what needs to be done and what order and how you do that.

Archie's description of the "calculated decisions" that must be made on the football field suggests he learned certain higher-order thinking skills while competing in college football that are transferable to other learning contexts and life experiences. He also discussed how playing college football helped him learn and understand "the importance of teamwork" and how, in order to succeed in life, he had to be able and willing to work with and seek help from others who knew what they are talking about and doing, "whatever subject matter it is."

Archie has successfully applied this concept of teamwork to his non-profit organization. With the driving force being his own story as a college athlete, its mission is to "coach young student athletes to aim for success off the field, off the track, off the court, whatever the case may be." To help "develop life and social skills of young student athletes between the ages of ten and thirteen, no matter what the career path may be," he assembled a great team of coaches, consultants, program coordinators, mentors, and volunteers to work with him in serving these athletes and achieving the mission of his organization. He explained,

> [W]e partner with major universities and their athletic departments. We train their collegiate athletes on a curriculum and they go out there to the elementary and middle schools and lead those sessions as head coaches and assistant coaches in the classroom.

Before founding this organization in 2013 and incorporating it and going full-time a few years later, Archie worked in "HR for the local school district, intentionally sought to build relationships here in [name of city] and learn about the education system." He discussed how he could have used his social network ties to pursue more lucrative career opportunities "but I knew that my purpose was to empower others, and this is one of the ways I'm going to make a difference. We're making a difference." Archie and his team continue to slowly but surely expand his organization and its programs nationally so that it can have impact beyond the local level.

Archie's recommendations for college sport leaders and other educational stakeholders interested in improving the educational experiences and outcomes of Black male athletes in particular focused on a few things. For one, he advocated for doing an inventory of these athletes' interests and assets by intentionally exposing them to different things that can "help them make decisions on possible tracks that they can go to" beyond playing professional sport. According to Archie, "So we know the track to make it to the NFL, but what is the track to be an attorney? What is the track to be a principal? What is the track to be a COO?" When asked if he had people who helped him explore various tracks he could pursue during his time as a college athlete, Archie said, "[W]e definitely had some career, academic advisers. They were more focused on making sure you got your degree. So that was great . . . but not necessarily the thought process of connecting you with some people who would really put me in the game of life."

Archie also emphasized the need for athletes to understand the platform they have, particularly in this age of social media, and use it to build meaningful relationships with key stakeholders during their playing days that can benefit them after their playing days are over. He expressed some frustration with how Black athletes at HWCU often allow themselves to be used without getting proper return on the investment they've made in these athletic programs:

> There's so much skills, other life skills for them to be successful outside of just catching a football and blocking for a university . . . It's really frustrating to see a lot of my peers and just Black athletes in general pretty much being used . . . You're being used for entertainment. There's a hundred thousand people in the audience; ninety-eight thousand of them don't look like you, don't come from the same resources. Well, probably a thousand of them could hire you and give you a $70,000 job tomorrow if they wanted to. And so making sure that they understand the importance of good relationships, how to conduct yourself, build relationships and then finding out who to build relationships with coming to it.

Archie was very intentional during his college playing days about treating people right, be it the janitor in his building or the chancellor of the university, and establishing and maintaining important relationships that helped him going forward. He shared how such social network ties helped him get donated office space for his organization on the campus of his alma mater. He provided a great example of how his intentionality in building and fostering these relationships during his playing days convinced people to buy into and support the work his organization was doing with young athletes:

> So the guy who was . . . head of media relations here was on my board . . . my former coach is on my board . . . so we use his influence to help push the movement forward. He's giving his time as well. So yeah, if

you don't treat people right and you don't maintain relationships, and if I didn't do it, they wouldn't be in my corner like they are.

JOHN: "DISCOVERING WHO I AM WITHOUT THE BALL IN MY HAND"

I guess the larger issue, the larger challenge and what's on my mind, is just . . . just given the climate of where we are in America socially, I think you have to be aware and be educated. That's something that I always think about, especially in my role as a learning specialist because I'm dealing with young Black males . . . So just trying to make sure that they understand the importance of being educated and being aware . . . just making sure you're conscious, making sure that you understand what all is happening in today's society and how that pertains to you . . . For me it's been interesting because . . . being a former college athlete and [thinking back on] my past, and then you talk about where we are as a society, you think about the role of college athletics and how it looks.

John's opening comments suggest that in light of the racially volatile climate that has been created—or more accurately, resurrected in the lead-up to and aftermath of the 2016 US presidential election, the education of Black male college athletes at HWCU is all the more important today and into the future. When I interviewed him, John was working as a learning specialist in a major Division I college sport program at an HWCU. He described life itself as a "giant school to me" and education as "a lifelong endeavor" that involves "being able to think critically about a situation or what have you and then being able to problem solve." He strongly believed that Black male college athletes' becoming educated involves their ability to understand the broader societal context and make sense of how it all relates to them. John's past experiences as a Black male college athlete had a significant impact on why he became a learning specialist and also influences how he works with Black male athletes today.

John was first introduced to and began playing football at the age of six. Born and raised in the South, he was "really heavily involved in sports" until he moved up North with his family during the latter stages of elementary school. He discussed how this move and new environment changed him and impacted his schooling experiences: "I remember going to my first class and people would say I talk funny and didn't fit in, being southern and stuff; so I became a knucklehead—like, my grades had started slipping a little bit." John felt that the "whole bunch of square people" in his new environment did not understand him or his struggle. This, combined with his being in the early stages of adolescence where "the hormones start kicking in" and "you start trying to puff your chest out a little bit" contributed to his loss of interest in school and his decision to "skip school and cut class." His rebellion against school caused discord between John and his stepfather, who was "like, 'If you don't read a book, you're not going to play football.'" This threat further exacerbated John's rebellious attitude, and he "stopped playing football when I was in middle school." It would not be until his sophomore year in high school that he would play football again.

John attended an international middle school where he had a "diverse type education," which included several foreign language classes. He attended a college preparatory high school, but his rebelliousness and academic struggles continued into his first couple of years there. In reflecting on this time in his life, John shared how his poor academic performance greatly disappointed his mother, and this is when he began to realize the need for change:

> . . . So my grade point—I didn't even play football—my grade point average my first semester was like a .9. It was a .9 . . . my teachers would be like, "He's educated enough to do it, but is just not putting effort in." And that's what I brought with me to high school and it bit me in the butt, especially when I started skipping class. And I remember bringing my report card home to my mom and my mom just looked at it, and was just like, I think that killed me . . . at that point I felt like I let her down so bad. And she was like, "This is all you want to be in your life? Then I'm not going to fight you on it." And I remember that conversation still to this day.

His mother's reaction is what "kind of like sparked something and lit a fire under me." It prompted John to focus on getting his grades up and engaging more with his teachers. The opportunity to eventually play football again became that proverbial "carrot on a stick" for John to get his act together as a student.

During his sophomore year in high school, John began to really turn things around and focus on school and his grades. He met a Black male teacher who tutored him in math during lunch and after school, and who also was one of the football coaches at the high school. John expressed his great appreciation for the significant amount of time this teacher and coach invested in him, and the critical role he played as a role model and mentor for John to look up to and talk to about different things related to life, school, and football. John "ended up going out and playing football when I was on academic probation." He started out playing junior varsity as a sophomore, "but then ended up playing varsity towards the end of my sophomore year." It was during his junior year that he "had a breakout season" as a linebacker and running back. Moreover, his grades slowly began to rise from the .9 grade point average of his freshman year to just under a 3.0 going into his senior year.

However, it was also during this breakout season that his mom, whom John described as "the cornerstone in our family" who "worked three jobs" to support his siblings and him, was diagnosed with a devastating autoimmune disease. By that point, John's stepfather and mother had divorced, and his mother decided to move to another city to be closer to John's sisters while she sought care for her illness. As the oldest boy, John stayed back and assumed the role of "man of the house" and caretaker for his younger brother while playing football and finishing his senior year of high school. It was also during this period that he started to be recruited and expressed great interest in learning more about the process of earning a scholarship to play Division I football. John described himself as a "dark horse recruit because people didn't really know about me because I just came out of nowhere." Many of the major FBS schools from the top Division I conferences in the nation did not show interest in him until the one he eventually went to saw his raw athleticism on film. After his senior season, this college offered him a scholarship to play defensive back—even though this was a position that he literally learned to play once he got there.

John shared with me how, unlike at other programs, the coaching staff at this Division I school expressed interest in visiting his ailing mother, and they were "the only school to be like 'Hey, you can take a year off and be with your family and we'll still honor your scholarship; the next year you come in with the next year's recruitment class.'" In addition, this particular school "ranked [academically] higher than" the other schools that were recruiting him, and the coaching staff's emphasis on "the academic piece of the school" during their recruitment visit impressed John's mother. In fact, even though John strongly considered going to a school that was much closer to his mother, it was she, along with one of the elders in his church, who convinced him to go away for college so that he could "become a man" and grow into "who I'm supposed to be."

When I asked John how playing college football at this particular HWCU helped contribute to his education as a young Black male, he responded, "I feel like [name of school] is where it happened." He discussed how "it was just a complete culture shock" coming to this HWCU, especially given that he "came from an all-Black neighborhood . . . the only White people I had in my neighborhood were cops, and we didn't like them." John shared how from the very first day when he was moving in, he was stereotyped not only because he was Black, but also because of how he dressed—the tall tees, Girbaud jeans, hoodie sweatshirts, Timberland boots, and Nike Air Force 1 shoes that are typically associated with the Hip Hop culture. He got suspicious looks from or was ill-treated by his White student peers. For example, people would cross the street to avoid him while walking on campus, or females would clutch their purses tight when he and his Black teammates got on elevators in dorms. This stereotyping extended into the classroom as well. John provided the example of a time when "I wrote a really good paper and my professor and the teaching assistant didn't believe I wrote it." John's experiences with being stereotyped as a Black male college athlete are similar to those discussed by the Black male athletes featured in the chapter 2 case study.

Although John's initial experiences at this HWCU were riddled with instances of being stereotyped, he did share how certain relationships he established with key people early on had a profound impact on him. John's early struggles in high school, coupled with the kind of high school he came from, moved the academic support staff in athletics to assign him to a learning specialist in his first year. This specialist was "a hippie White dude" who "just challenged me on ways of thinking and introduced me to different things." John acknowledged that on the surface, they did not seem to have anything in common, "but that was my guide." This specialist would engage John in "deep conversations" about the meaning of life and introduced him to various possibilities in life beyond playing football and making a lot of money; for example, he discussed what it means to pursue and obtain a PhD. He also helped John improve his writing and encouraged him to take advantage of various lectures and other learning opportunities on campus outside athletics and the classroom setting. Unlike many of his teammates who decided to play or were encouraged by the coaching staff to play their first year in the program, John's conscious decision to redshirt his freshman year contributed to his ability to attend such events.

John's experience at this HWCU was also enriched by the Black male graduate student who ran the study table for the football team and exposed him to important Black history (e.g., the Black Panther Party movement). John's conversations and interactions with these educational stakeholders helped raise his level of critical consciousness and awareness to a place that was different than most of his Black male teammates.

I asked John if he thought playing his first year instead of redshirting would have changed the trajectory of his educational experiences. He acknowledged that although he went to that HWCU with the mind-set that "school was going to come first regardless," had he been asked to or made the decision to play right away, "I would have probably been more football-oriented." Interestingly, he further stated, "I would have had more respect for coaches and the whole process, and I don't think I would have been able to think as deeply as I do now . . . but because I didn't play, it gave me the opportunity to reflect, to think."

Once John completed his redshirt year, he was in a position to compete for a starting position as a defensive back going into his second year in the program. However, as has been the case for so many other Black male college athletes, including many who are featured in this book, the injury bug bit John hard. Going into the last day of fall camp practice, John seemed poised to secure a starting position at defensive back when he "ended up . . . fracturing my left foot." Prior to this devastating injury and in the lead-up to the season, his confidence was riding high. He believed, "I can do this, I'm going to the NFL." Given his mother's illness and his desire to play the minimum required number of years to be eligible for the NFL draft and then use football "to get this money for my mom," this made the injury all the more difficult to accept. And to make matters worse, he was already homesick when this injury happened.

Although academics were important to John and the redshirt year helped him transition into college life, he second-guessed his decision to redshirt and shared how his mind-set in the aftermath of this injury was, "I shouldn't have redshirted; I should have just played, then I would have already had the starting position locked up." He recalled, "I just remember being hurt [literally and figuratively], man" when this injury happened. Similar to Bobby (chapter 2), Archie, and other Black male college athletes whose playing careers are derailed by injury or do not end on their own terms, John revealed how he "went through a deep depression." He also shared that none of the coaches came up to the hospital to visit him after his injury. They did not really check on him, even though he stayed away from the athletics facilities for a long time after getting out of the hospital. John missed almost two full seasons, but he worked very hard to come back from an injury his doctors thought was not possible to overcome. He became a leader on special teams during his junior season. However, there were other injury setbacks, including damage to his hamstring, and with younger players in front of him on the depth chart at his position, he was never really given the opportunity to fulfill the potential that the head coach who recruited him had seen. This coach abruptly retired before John's first injury, but instead of learning of this directly from the coach, John and his teammates first heard the news on ESPN. Like other Black males featured in this chapter, John experiences as a college athlete at a HWCU helped him realize just "how much of a business college athletics is."

John's injuries and their aftermath became "the defining moment for me in regards to who am I without a ball in my hand." The sobering reality for him was that "football is fleeting" and "that's when I realized, 'Hell, you really need to be ready for when it's over.'" This is when he decided to put "my confidence in my academic side" and visited an assistant dean, who he described as an "old Black dude with a suit on with some tennis shoes." This Black male educator engaged John in deep and meaningful conversations about race and other related topics, and challenged him to think critically, particularly about his history as a Black man in America. Barack Obama's historical election and first years in office took place during John's time on campus, and made these conversations around race all the more important and relevant.

The assistant dean, who also was a former college athlete, helped John to explore and figure out what he should major in and study, which ended up being history. Between this assistant dean, the learning specialist, and the graduate student who ran the study table, John had mentors and role models who helped expand his horizons and expose him to critical readings, events, and ideas that greatly enhanced his educational experiences as an athlete at this HWCU. More than the football coaching staff or athletics administrators, it was these educators in the academic domain who had the greatest influence on John's educational experiences and outcomes. Their influence is why John became a learning specialist and has aspirations to be a "change agent" and continue working directly and "building positive relationships with college athletes and watching them develop into extraordinary people."

The profound impact that John's interactions and relationships with these three educators had on him also impacted many of his teammates. John was being exposed to knowledge his teammates and he were not seeing or getting in the football program, and John began engaging them in conversations about this knowledge. As one of the few Black players on the team who had over a 3.0 grade point average, his teammates started referring to him as "the grandpa on the team" and "pastor."

John also revealed how because he was sharing what he was learning with his teammates and "used to wear black [clothes] all the time," people in the football program suspected or "thought I was a Black Panther." Certain coaches would indirectly try to ask if this was the case by inquiring about "if I'm like politically involved with any organizations and stuff." This story reminds me in some ways of one of the Black male football athletes I used to mentor in the SUPER bridge program (see chapter 1). After deep conversations about race, I remember giving this athlete a video of an interview of Malcolm X (who only went to the eighth grade in formal schooling) successfully debating and schooling White male Ivy League–educated journalists about race matters. This athlete then took the video to the football facilities to share with his teammates. Similar to John's experience, this did not go over too well with the coaching staff.

As I ended our provocative conversation, I asked John to provide thoughts and recommendations for how decision makers and other key stakeholders in college sport can help improve the relationship between Black male athletes' participation in college sport and their educational experiences and outcomes. First and foremost, John believed, you have to get them out of the silo of big-time college sport and "expose them to stuff" beyond the playbook, competition, and the athletic department. He reflected on how his exposure to learning specialists and other academic support personnel, university administrators, faculty, and other key stakeholders across campus was crucial to the broadening of his worldview and development of critical thinking skills. He suggested that athletics administrators and coaches—who are primarily judged on wins and losses, not the holistic development of athletes—must be open to strategic partnerships across campus if they desire to effectively address the education of Black male athletes and their peers. John discussed a program he created during his time as a master's student where "the whole point of it was holistic student-athlete development." They would meet in different spaces throughout campus outside athletics and expose athletes to Black law school students, speakers from outside campus, and others who could help "broaden their worldview." He also discussed a mentoring program he set up in the local schools, where many of the Black athletes would work with P–12 students. This had such a powerful impact on some of his teammates that "they ended up becoming teachers because of it." John looked back on how the presence of his Black male math teacher and tutor made all the difference in the world for him when he was struggling early on as a high school student. Both the academic and popular literature has called for more Black male teachers in P–12 schools because of their potentially important role and function in the education of young Black boys in particular and students more generally.[13]

Related to his first recommendation, John also said he would like to see the creation of more culturally relevant programs that teach Black male athletes about themselves and the skills they need to "know how to take care of themselves than to just have a degree that they don't know how to use" and apply to life going forward. The Collective Uplift program, which was founded by Joseph Cooper at the University of Connecticut, is an example of a culturally relevant program that was designed to do what John has suggested is needed on these HWCU campuses.[14] Furthermore, John stressed that instead of labeling Black male athletes as "at-risk" and focusing on their weaknesses or so-called deficiencies, educators at these HWCU need to "meet the student where he or she is at . . . maybe they're not good at certain things, but find out what they are good at and try to tailor a program around their strengths." As mentioned in the introduction, scholars have discussed the importance of taking an asset- and strength-based approach to working with Black students and other students of color instead of a deficit approach.[15] The following quote captures the essence of how John thinks about and approaches his work with Black male athletes who many people in athletics write off and view as irredeemable:

We had a student come in one time and everybody was, like "Man, this dude's a loss" . . . And he was hard. He came in low-functioning; came in from a terrible school system; and had horrible character issues. I mean, he was hard. People couldn't deal with him. I loved it—I was like, "Give him to me." And he was doing the same. Unfortunately, he didn't make it all the way at [name of school where John works] because he ended up transferring, but the same kid that they kind of were, like, "This kid will never be more than this," he's at another school and he got a 3.0. So you know what I mean? So what is it? Is it he can't do it or is because you thought he couldn't do it?

EJ: COLLEGE SPORT AS A PLATFORM TO DISCOVER YOUR "WHY"

[W]hen I think about college sports, because I was an athlete playing on the college level and now I work in the administration, I've seen both sides. And so now I said, "OK, now that I know both sides, what is my purpose? What am I trying to accomplish?" Because just like any former athlete, you always have an opportunity to go in a few different direction . . . coaching, academics, whatever it may be. This profession, this area of interest, sports in general will give you a platform that people who don't play sports may not necessarily have . . . And I think from the time that you are a student athlete, you start to become an expert in something because you work on it so much—you know, your sport—and because in sport you learn certain skill sets. It's like teamwork and work ethic and resilience that is unique to this profession, this area. Sports provide a different level of pressure . . . it tests you in ways that you may not normally get in another profession. And then you do it repetitively, so you become, this becomes kind of who you are.

At the time we spoke, EJ was working as a senior-level leader in academic support for a major FBS program at a HWCU. Throughout our conversation, it was clear that he viewed Black male athletes' participation in college sport as something that could and should be leveraged to positively contribute to their educational experiences and outcomes. His sentiment that "you start to become an expert at something" when you have played organized school sport all the way up to the college level speaks to the great power and potential of sport to contribute to the education of Black males like him. In fact, this thirty-one-year-old former college football wide receiver turned doctoral student and senior-level academic counselor believed that college athletes should actually have the option to pursue their sport as an academic major, especially since they put so much time into mastering their specific sport (e.g., football players learning complicated schemes and applying them to play) and developing skills, like math, that are transferable to other contexts. EJ stated, "I think you have to have a major in sport . . . because there's a science to it . . . you may not realize it, but you're as precise as a surgeon might be in studying football." In supporting his claim, he mentioned the television show *Sport Science*, which originally aired in 2007 and explores the science and engineering underlying athletic endeavors. Educational psychology scholar David Pragman has long advocated for this idea of a college major in sport performance with a specialization in the sport chosen by athletes.[16] In line with this thinking, EJ suggested that by allowing college athletes this option, "it might make you a better player because you're thinking about mechanics now" and that this could actually "provide an advantage for a team if they really took it seriously." He maintained that a formalized academic major or specialization in sport could help make athletes better students of the game and potentially better students in the classroom and beyond.

EJ was born and attended elementary and middle school in the Southwest. Interestingly, although he "was always a relatively good athlete" and played "recreation ball," EJ did not play organized school sport until he got to high school, which is not typical for most athletes who end up playing Division I college sports. EJ attributed his late start in interscholastic sports to his parents. EJ's parents were not together when he was growing up. He lived with his mother during his early childhood into adolescence, and she "just didn't like or promote sports" because she did not want EJ to get hurt. EJ further shared how his dad, who he has been "very close" to throughout his life, wanted him to focus more on his academics. According to EJ,

> I would visit my dad over the summer, and so when I was ready to move with my dad, my dad's first priority was to make sure I was good academically . . . So he's, like, "I don't want you playing any sports, I want you to focus on school." So I did my best to be good at school because I really wanted to play . . . When I moved to [city where his

father lived] after my freshman year, my dad said "OK, I'll let you run cross-country. That will ease you into the sports world."

EJ's father, who also played high school and college football, continued to allow him to participate in track in his sophomore and junior years. It was not until his senior year that EJ's father allowed him to play football. In fact, this would be the first time he ever put on a helmet "because I didn't even play, like, Pee Wee."

Because he got such a late start playing organized football and essentially "learned football from senior year really all through college," EJ was not heavily recruited coming out of high school. He received two offers, one from a Division I program not in the FBS and the other from an FCS program at an HBCU. He ended up accepting a football scholarship to the Division I program at a HWCU. Although he played defensive back (safety and corner) in his lone season in high school and was recruited at that position by these two college programs, EJ "got switched around a bunch of times, and then I was, like, to my coach, "Let me just play receiver." He redshirted his first year and played three years on special teams before he finally "started my last year at [name of university]." As he was working his way up the depth chart at his position, the teammate in front of him was injured, "so I stepped in and started from then on." EJ graduated that next summer and then decided to transfer and play his final season of college football at a comparable Division I program. He continued to progress as a starting wide receiver and "had a really good season" before being invited to the rookie camp for an NFL team. However, the NFL did not work out for EJ, so he moved on to pursue his graduate education and career path to becoming a leader in college athletics administration.

Given that EJ picked up and learned football so late compared with most his peers, I was interested to know if he saw educational value in teaching himself the sport at the end of high school and throughout his college playing career. His immediate response was "Absolutely, yes!" EJ discussed how not only was he "learning football on the fly," but perhaps most importantly, he was "dealing with the environment" that is college sport and the harsh reality that even if you work hard to be good, "it may not pay off like you think it should." He further shared that "what I didn't realize is that what I was doing was going to set me up for how I operated later on in life. So to me, that's the educational value." EJ acknowledged, "I could not be doing what I'm doing right now if I didn't develop the skills that I developed in high school and college" as a football player. He largely credited the knowledge and insight he gained learning and playing college sport with helping him in his role as a senior-level leader in academic support.

When asked to further reflect on the role his participation in college sport played in his education, which he defined as "gaining an accurate knowledge of things that affect your life," EJ shared some interesting perspectives. In particular, he discussed how his Black teammates and he were not really exposed to broader social issues, and this forced them "to do extra" to learn more about "what's going on outside my day-to-day" activities as a football player at this HWCU. However, according to EJ, when Black male athletes take such initiatives to extend their learning beyond sport participation, this might prompt the coaching staff or others in the program to view them as "anti-establishment." EJ shared how Black male college athletes often "are being overseen by individuals who might not necessarily understand or care" why they might want to pursue educational opportunities outside their sport (e.g., pledge a fraternity) or learn more about broader social issues, and perhaps even engage in activist activities in this Colin Kaepernick–inspired fourth wave of athlete activism. EJ stated that such educational pursuits are too often "either discouraged or maybe not promoted" by the power elite in college sport.

EJ shared how when he was playing college football his Black teammates and he were fairly conscious of things going on around them:

> [T]he group of guys I played with were very aware of what was going on, how we were treating it, and why we were treating it that way. We might have been totally off base on some things because we were young and emotional. But there are other things that I see now that we were right on for.

As an example, EJ discussed "the plantation type of atmosphere or aura that you get from playing in college football." This description of college football at HWCU ties into the reference I made in the introduction to sociologist and sport studies scholar Billy Hawkin's theorization of Division I college football and basketball programs at HWCU as "the new plantation." These programs, according to Hawkins, too often partake in the colonization of the Black male body in the name of providing educational opportunities via the athletic scholarship and sport participation at these prominent institutions of higher education.[17] When asked how his teammates and he navigated this space during their playing days, EJ answered,

> [I]t forced me to find out like who I was; it forced me to be more self-aware; it forced me to think about how am I going to deal with this? Some of my teammates were upset. Some of them acted out. Some of them stayed to themselves. Some of them just said, "I'm going to focus on me; I'm not going to worry about nothing else." And some of them just became more educated.

EJ did mention that how Black male athletes chose to deal with or respond to their colonization "also coincides with how much you're playing." This suggests that athletes who are starting or playing a lot might not be as inclined to challenge or push back against the system, even if that system is not helping them or other Black male athletes become more well-rounded, better people.

Although EJ described college sport as a "plantation type of atmosphere," he acknowledged that participation in big-time college sport does potentially provide a platform unlike any other for Black male athletes "to build their brand" and pursue life opportunities. However, he made it clear that Black males do not need to play college sport to be successful in life: "There's too much of that talk, too much of that culture in college athletics, as if we need this . . . and that's when I say the . . . slave mentality [is prevalent]." EJ expressed frustration with this mind-set of athletes and other stakeholders in big-time college sport that the field and court are the single or primary avenues for Black males to succeed in life. In pondering why this mind-set exists, he questioned whether "there is a separation between multimillion dollars and student development" in college sport and "if you can have both." He asserted, "There clearly is a discrepancy between what people say and what's actually happening" in college sport as it relates to the education of Black male athletes. EJ's suggestion that too much lip service but not enough action is expended toward the holistic development of football and basketball athletes made me reflect on a conversation I once had with a senior-level administrator who was in charge of academic support for athletics at a major Division I HWCU. She shared with me that her job was extremely difficult, if not impossible, because her focus was on human development, whereas the focus of her boss (the athletic director) was on commercial development. This example speaks to the challenges and contradictions associated with serving the educational interests and needs of Black male college athletes and their peers in this era of academic capitalism.

At the end of our discussion, I asked EJ what recommendations for change he would offer leaders and administrators who run and oversee college sport. After acknowledging this was "a tough question," EJ stated, "Well, I think that if you want to do it the right way, you have to look at it, you have to restructure how it's all done." When asked to elaborate on how this restructuring might look, EJ discussed how "everybody in the athletic department has a role" and responsibility that may or may not be for the direct benefit of college athletes (e.g., athletic directors focus heavily on fundraising). He insisted that it is important that people working in these different capacities begin to critically question *why* they do what they do and how it might genuinely promote the well-being of college athletes. EJ learned the importance of defining your core values and your "why" as a professional working in college sport during his participation in the NCAA leadership institute. He suggested that because "there's so much money involved" in college sport today, "nobody's really asking that question" about how their work roles and responsibilities are ultimately impacting the college athletes they should be serving.

EJ assumed that the people who plan, organize, control, and lead college sport do not have nefarious intentions in regard to the education of college athletes. To make his point, he referenced the academic-athletic scandal at the University of North Carolina at Chapel Hill that first came to light around 2010. It had been reported that several football and basketball players had been enrolled in questionable independent study classes—ironically enough, in the Department of African and Afro-American Studies department—designed primarily to keep them eligible, over the course of several years.[18] EJ stated, "I'm sure those people weren't trying to do that." He insisted that ethical matters such as academic scandals or questionable practices like clustering a large number of football and basketball athletes into a certain major or particular class unfold because "people overlook the reality of a situation" and fail to ask, "Why are we doing this and what impact is it going to have?" EJ was adamant that if leaders and educators in college sport are not diligent about asking why they do certain things and how their actions and decisions might impact the education of college athletes, they are headed in the wrong direction. This is why, from EJ's perspective, as a professional working in athletics, "you have to constantly really self-monitor, self-check, especially when you're in a position in these systems to effectuate change."

Another pertinent issue raised regarding reform in college sport was whether or not the people working in the area of academic support for athletics are adequately prepared and "as emotionally intelligent in this profession as they should be" to work effectively with Black male athletes and their peers. EJ discussed how people often lack "the formal training or their personality is not a fit" to effectively address the interests and needs of the athletes they work with. For example, in regard to formal training or expertise he observed how learning specialists often do not come from special education backgrounds or academic counselors do not have a counseling degree. But from EJ's perspective, if the leaders who are hiring and working with these staff members are diligent about defining their core values and their why "they're developing their staff, and those individuals who may not be experts, trained experts, are better equipped to help the student."

In regard to academic support personnel having the personality or background to effectively understand and work with athletes, particularly Black males in the high-profile sports of football and basketball, EJ expressed that professionals who do not come from the same or similar racial background as these Black male athletes "have limitations" as to what they can do to impact these athletes in the four to five years they have to work with them. Similar to the recommendations of the Black male athletes from the case study in chapter 2, EJ's sentiments suggest the need for more Black and other racial minority professionals in the area of academic support for athletics at HWCU.

As we concluded our interview, EJ and I discussed how he views his role in his position as a senior academic counselor for football, and the approach he takes in handling the sometimes different priorities other stakeholders and he might have regarding the education of college athletes. He created a visual framework (see figure 3.1) to illustrate a continuum of the potential measures of success for college athletes over time, and provided an example

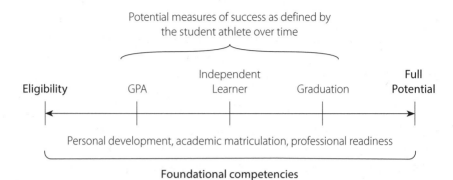

FIGURE 3.1   Potential measures of success as defined by the student athlete over time

of how he would approach a situation with a coach whose only or primary goal is to keep athletes eligible to play their sport. EJ uses eligibility as the starting point for measuring how successfully he is doing his job, but ultimately, his focus is on working with athletes to help them fulfill their full potential and reach certain benchmarks toward educational empowerment. For him, educational empowerment "falls wherever the student-athlete is ready." EJ discussed how the Black male athletes he works with come to him with a "wide range of ability and motivation," but he is always pushing each of them "to help you reach a goal as close to your potential as possible." He is constantly trying to get these athletes to see they have more in them, and used his own personal experience as a college athlete to put an exclamation point by stating, "Because that's what happened to me. And then when I realized, man, I can do anything I want to do, then I was able to start my PhD program, do the things that are tough. Like I was never a 3.0, 4.0 guy, but I felt like I had more I could do."

DISCUSSION AND CONCLUSION

The narratives of these nine former Black male college athletes tell powerful stories of excellence and resilience. From their early childhood through P–12 schooling into and beyond their college sport participation at Division I HWCU, each of them faced various challenges and struggles. They recognized the importance of education and the role it played in creating opportunities for them in life beyond college sport participation. Collectively, they defined education as:

- The accumulation of life experiences, the lifelong acquisition of accurate and proper knowledge about particular subjects/topics/issues, and the application or use of this knowledge and experience as a tool to help solve problems and create life opportunities for self and others
- The ability to think critically about and to learn how to effectively navigate social, political, and cultural challenges in this White-dominated society
- The process of gaining a certain level of consciousness and curiosity about oneself, others around them, and the world at large

All nine Black males acknowledged that the completion of certain basic courses in a curriculum and graduation with a high school diploma and a college degree are an important part of the education process. However, as my summary of their conceptualizations of education suggests, these former athletes viewed true and real education for Black male athletes as much more than just going to school and graduating.

The narratives presented in this chapter reveal that these athletes' participation in college sport at the various HWCU they attended yielded significant benefits and contributed in meaningful ways to their education. First, several of them explicitly mentioned how their college sport participation helped them establish a reliable framework or system they use to this day to organize, prepare, problem-solve, and make decisions in their daily life. Effective time-management skills, discipline, work ethic, resilience, and teamwork are all things that many of them directly attributed to their participation in college sport. Second, the improvement of higher-order thinking and study skills was a noteworthy educational outcome that emerged from my interviews with these Black males. For example, the analysis and breakdown of practice and game film was a skill set these athletes were able to transfer to the classroom and other life endeavors beyond the playing field and court. Third, these Black males acknowledged that college sport participation also gave them high visibility and a powerful platform to build their brands. College sport provided them access to learning experiences and life opportunities that allowed them to achieve social mobility in the form of strong social network ties and relationships and career options. Finally, and perhaps most interestingly, some of these Black males shared how redshirting their first year and/or early retirement from college sport created opportunities to develop critical consciousness and establish meaningful relationships with key educational stakeholders both within (e.g., learning specialists) and outside (e.g., assistant dean, faculty) the athletics department. These Black males had profound doubts about whether they would have been able to develop critical awareness and establish such impactful relationships had they fully immersed themselves in the day-to-day activities and culture of the athletics program. In addition, their exposure to key role models (e.g., Willis's Black head football coach, and Black leaders in the broader community this coach exposed his players to) and engagement in various activities beyond athletics (e.g., guest lectures on campus) had great educative value, particularly because they helped these Black males develop interests and identities beyond the athlete role.

Although their participation in college sport contributed in meaningful ways to these Black males' education, there were also various matters that limited and inhibited the potential educational value of their college sport participation. From a macro-level standpoint, these Black males became increasingly cognizant of the fact that college sport is a "big business" and is governed by an academic capitalist model and mind-set that relegates Black male athletes to the role of expendable parts in a system that was not necessarily designed to prioritize their education. Marc's concerns about the athletics industrial complex and how it influences the decision making of leaders is a case in point. Marc criticized how the "market" dictates decisions such as the exorbitant amount of money head football and basketball coaches are paid and how much power and influence these coaches are given over athletes and the athletic department more generally. He lamented the unchecked power of coaches at these HWCU, and insisted this can create situations where these athletes feel compelled to capitulate to the market-driven agenda of these coaches in the bubble or silo that big-time college sport often is or creates. Such systems and structures could certainly stifle or kill the curiosity of Black male athletes.

This stifling of Black male athletes' curiosity often starts early in life as they move along the conveyor belt from youth sport into college sport. A few of the athletes interviewed alluded to this notion of the athlete seasoning complex, and how a misplaced focus on athletic identity by Black male youth can set them up for academic failure or great struggle once they arrive on the campuses of HWCU. The single-minded pursuit of athletic goals and aspirations oftentimes moves Black male athletes to engage in self-limiting behaviors that do not necessarily serve their overall educational interests and development. This behavior can be exacerbated in the cultures of low academic expectations that often exist in the athletic programs at HWCU.

The Black males featured in this chapter offered several important recommendations to improve the educational experiences and outcomes of Black male college athletes at HWCU. At the broader, structural level, they suggested leaders and educational professionals should:

- Focus more on critically examining and "fixing" harmful organizational cultures, policies, and practices so that the inner gifts and talents of Black male athletes can be properly nurtured; in other words, take a strengths-based approach to working with athletes, as opposed to a deficit approach
- Engage in a critical self-assessment of why they are doing the work they do, and to what extent they have the preparation and capacity to serve the educational interests and needs of Black male athletes
- Conduct an inventory or needs assessment at the beginning of Black male athletes' careers, and engage them in meaningful dialogue throughout their time on campus to learn more about and address their assets, interests, wants, needs, and values
- Provide Black male athletes a real and permanent seat at the table to discuss matters related to their education
- Learn, embrace, and engage in culturally relevant pedagogy and provide culturally relevant programs and activities to serve the interests and needs of Black male athletes
- Stop making human development ancillary to capital development
- Integrate athletics into the broader university setting and develop strategic partnerships across campus
- Consistently expose Black male athletes to people, places, ideas, and activities outside athletics and beyond campus
- Hire more Black professionals in the area of academic support for athletics and other leadership roles

- Consider hiring academic support personnel in athletics (e.g., learning specialists, academic counselors) who have formal training in specialized areas such as special education or counseling psychology
- Explore the feasibility of college athletes having an option to formally study their sport as an official academic major
- Focus on better understanding and closing the gap in the transfer of Black male athlete competence from the playing field and court to the classroom and other learning contexts

At the individual level, they suggested Black male athletes should:

- Take control of their own educational experiences and opportunities; for example, make it a priority to explore the vast resources these HWCU have to offer beyond the athletic department
- Learn about the concept of degree plans, and chose to take classes that will challenge and set themselves up for success in life
- Build and maintain important relationships and social networks
- Understand and use the platform they have, particularly in this era of social media

Many of these recommendations align well with those discussed in the academic literature. I focus on this more in chapter 4.

CHAPTER 4

Conclusion

But because black athletes' academic problems are in large part rooted in and intertwined with black youths' societal circumstances more generally there can be no effective resolution of the educational circumstances of black athletes at any academic level except in coordination with commensurate efforts in society.

Harry Edwards[1]

Organizations are the key intermediaries between the larger society and the lives of individuals and groups. They typically mirror the larger society and are in the position of either passing on or sometimes challenging dominant patterns and their effects . . . While the people and groups in an organization work together for overarching goals and purposes, they also have different interests—based on their identity, role, functional unit—and these interest groups often compete for limited resources.

Mark Chesler, Amanda E. Lewis, and James E. Crowfoot[2]

Stereotypes of a Black male misunderstood, and it's still all good.

The Notorious B.I.G.[3]

T HE CENTRAL AIM OF *Race, Sports, and Education* was to address the question, *What does college sport have to do with the education of Black male athletes?* That is, how and in what ways does Black males' participation in Division I football and basketball programs at HWCU influence their educational opportunities and outcomes? The varied and unique voices and experiences of the Black males represented in chapters 2 and 3 provided important insight into improving opportunities and outcomes for Black male college athletes. The collective stories of these Black males reveal that on the one hand they certainly reaped important benefits—including access to institutions of higher education and travel opportunities—and many positive educational outcomes from their participation in college sport. In particular, it helped prepare them for success in both their personal and professional lives. They shared how playing NCAA Division I sports at HWCU helped them establish a useful organizational framework or system for problem solving and decision making in their daily life and work, improve their higher-order thinking and study skills, gain high visibility and a platform for achieving social mobility, and build meaningful relationships and establish strong social networks. On the other hand, these Black males were also critically aware of how racism, athletic department cultures, NCAA policies and other various historical, systemic, and structural forces and matters in college sport restricted opportunities to pursue true education. They recognized the myriad challenges associated with navigating the hyper-commercialized world of Division I college sport at HWCU.

I begin this chapter by providing a working framework on how particular macro-, meso-, and micro-level factors or matters interact to influence educational opportunities, experiences, and outcomes for Black male college athletes. Second, I discuss relevant research, policy, and practical implications. I include policy and practical recommendations for leaders and professional practitioners in higher education and college sport, as well as those leaders and practitioners in secondary education who are in a position to help prepare Black male athletes for higher education. In conclusion, I challenge current and future Black male athletes in Division I football and basketball programs at HWCU to critically reflect on the narratives in chapters 2 and 3 and engage with this book's practical and theoretical content to inform their decision-making on how to best navigate the world of college sport.

TOWARD A FRAMEWORK ON BLACK MALE ATHLETE EDUCATION MATTERS

The purpose of this section is not necessarily to present a comprehensive framework that fully captures all the complexities of Black male athletes' educational opportunities, experiences, and outcomes (see Joseph Cooper's book *From Exploitation Back to Empowerment* for a more detailed examination and analysis).[4] Instead, I use it to highlight important factors that interact to influence educational opportunities, experiences, and outcomes of Black male athletes and their peers. More specifically, I discuss the elite White male dominance system at the macro-level; organizations as cultures, political systems, and instruments of domination at the meso level; and the prevalence and impact of racial stereotypes at the micro level.

Macro-Level Matters

Any meaningful discussion of education matters pertaining to Black male athletes is not possible without situating the conversation within broader historical and structural elements of US society and social institutions, with the emphasis on how these external elements often exert considerable influence on the lived experiences and life outcomes of Black male athletes. As the quote by Harry Edwards at the outset of this chapter connotes, discussions of Black male athletes' academic and other education matters should be understood within the context of broader "societal circumstances." In other words, we must critically interrogate and address problems that exist in the larger society if we are serious about providing effective (re)solutions to the "educational circumstances" facing Black male athletes in college sport and all levels of organized school sport. I argue that addressing educational issues and challenges Black male athletes face starts with understanding the elite White male dominance system that has undergirded US society from its very inception.

Joe Feagin and Kimberly Ducey describe elite White men as the central problem of the twenty-first century. These scholars draw from the work of scholars and activists in the Black radical tradition, particularly W. E. B. DuBois, to explicitly call out elite White male architects of the centuries-long inequality and oppression that has plagued Black people, other non-White people, women, and poor people from all racial and ethnic backgrounds. They describe the intertwined oppression subsystems of racism, sexism, and classism as a triple social helix, and that these subsystems have *codetermined* and *coreproduced* each other for centuries. They argue that the relatively few White males at the pinnacle of major US institutions form an oligarchy that rules society via their own actions and the actions of their acolytes. According to Feagin and Ducey,

> regularly, over short and long periods of time, they seek to protect and expand capitalistic profit and property, their position in the national and global racial hierarchy, and their hegemonic masculinity in the

global gender order . . . they are so powerful substantially because of the major networks and major organizations in which they are groomed, situated, and/or operative.[5]

As I suggested in the introduction, elite White men have long utilized their racial, gender, and class positions and framing to create and perpetuate systems of exploitation and dominance in and through college sport. Previous literature has not necessarily been explicit in naming the elite White male dominance system and calling out specific elite White men who have organized and controlled college sport in the past and present. However, scholars and other social commentators have acknowledged that this exploitative system has shaped college sport for decades. Moreover, they have discussed the deleterious influence this system of exploitation at both the societal and college sport levels has had on the education of Black male athletes in particular. For example, in a discussion of some prospects for the year 2020 in the book *Racism in College Athletics*, sport sociologist Stanley Eitzen states,

> African American athletes in big-time college athletic programs are part of two contexts, both of which disadvantage them. The first context is the interracial climate of US society. On every dimension related to health, housing, work, income/wealth, and education, African Americans, when compared to Whites, are disadvantaged . . . African American athletes recruited to big-time college programs are also part of a corporate/entertainment world. They are hired (for room, board, books, and tuition) to perform on the athletic fields and in the arenas to generate monies, media interest, and public relations for universities. They are recruited for their athletic talents but not necessarily for their intellectual abilities. Because African American athletes come disproportionately from economically, socially, and educationally disadvantaged backgrounds, the situation is loaded against them. From the perspective of many coaches and athletic administrators, these individuals are athletes first and only incidentally students.[6]

This quote speaks to the impact racism has had on Black people in US society in general, the educational system broadly, and more specifically, college sport. To Eitzen's point, leaders and stakeholders in higher education and college sport have too often treated Black male athletes at HWCU chiefly as the primary laborers or the main "products" who produce the entertainment spectacles on the fields and courts of play for various groups to enjoy and consume.[7] This is a point Willis (chapter 3) made when he suggested that leaders in college sport should "stop treating us like dollars" and only as "spectacles to be witnessed."

At the heart of critical race theory (CRT) and systemic racism theory (SRT) is the understanding that White-on-Black oppression is foundational and deeply embedded in the economic, legal, political, educational, and other social institutions in American society.[8] CRT pioneer Derrick Bell's notion of racial realism argues that racism is endemic and a permanent part of American society and its social history. More specifically, Bell realizes that Black people will always be hard-pressed to gain real equality in a White male patriarchal, racist, and capitalistic society like the US. He understood that the racial progress Blacks have made has been temporary or short-lived in the sense that racial patterns have always shifted and adapted to maintain White dominance and privilege.[9] For example, as I mentioned in chapter 1 and as Willis's narrative in chapter 3 suggested, Barack Obama's election was a sign of progress and great hope for a nation rooted in the elite White male dominance system. However, the election of Donald Trump as Obama's successor was a grim and sobering reminder of how social progress that symbolically and/or substantively benefits Blacks and other marginalized populations has typically been at the will and design of elite White males who decide if, when, how, and to what extent this progress will take shape.

The practice of putting policies and people in place within educational institutions to serve the interests of elite White males extends back decades. In the book *The White Architects of Black Education*, scholar William Watkins builds particularly on the work of W. E. B. DuBois and Carter G. Woodson to "investigate the ideological construct of colonial Black education by examining the views, politics, and practices of the White architects that funded, created, and refined it."[10] He focuses specifically on the (mis)deeds of wealthy and powerful White males who played pivotal roles in shaping Black education from the end of the Civil War up to the *Brown v. Board of Education* decision. Of particular note is General Samuel Chapman Armstrong, whom Watkins places at the center of his analysis.

According to Watkins, Armstrong's Hampton model was predicated on creating a new social order that moved away from the old form of colonization that relied on physical force, cruelty, and outright denial of human dignity during chattel slavery to one that recognized the need for new types of labor, markets, techniques, and social organization. Unlike some of his contemporaries, Armstrong was not in denial about Black peoples' intellectual capacity to learn. However, he still believed Blacks were barbaric and in need of character, morality, and socialization. Thus, his program of education and social organization focuses on civilizing, disciplining, and exploiting Black people in ways that made them nonthreatening to the elite White male dominance system, and serviceable to the interests of the elite. Armstrong and his colleagues played a critical role in the expansion of imperialism, the birth of Jim Crow, and the emergence of monopoly capitalism. These White males viewed Black people as central figures, particularly as laborers, in the global economic transformation that was taking place after the Reconstruction era into the early twentieth century.

Watkins is keenly aware that schooling, not an education designed to liberate them from White rule, is what Blacks have historically been subjected to in the US educational system. Indeed, there has been "too much schooling, too little education," as Mwalimu Shujaa has noted, which has stunted the development of many young Black males in this educational system.[11] I examined this idea in chapter 1 in my discussion of Tyrone Howard's notion of the athlete seasoning complex and William Rhoden's concept of the conveyor belt. This education matter was particularly problematic for some of the Black males whose narratives appear in chapter 3. The early socialization of young Black male athletes into a predominant athlete mind-set and role explains, at least in part, why we have witnessed cases of highly gifted Black male athletes such as James Brooks and Dexter Manley being pushed through P–12 education, and in some cases, through higher education despite the fact that they were functionally illiterate during and after their college and professional playing days.[12]

Cases such as these and the countless others raise some important questions: Are Black males recruited into these athletic programs at HWCU to be truly educated? Are they primarily recruited to serve as that "massive labor supply," as John Henrik Clarke argues (see chapter 1)? To what extent are Black male athletes being trained to serve the interests of the NCAA, HWCU, and other powerful stakeholder groups as opposed to being properly educated to serve their own interests and the interests of their communities? The literature as well as the narratives from some of the Black males highlighted in this book reveal the unfortunate reality that HWCU have historically been far more concerned with exploiting the athletic prowess of Black males than engaging them in educationally meaningful activities beyond sport and play. Scholars have employed Derrick Bell's interest-convergence principle to expose the business and political motives surrounding White power brokers' decisions to heavily recruit and consistently invite Black athletic talent to HWCU in the years after the *Brown v. Board of Education* decision.[13] Importantly, Jamel Donnor has analyzed legal cases involving Black male football and basketball athletes to demonstrate the presence of educational malpractice and breach of contract issues at these HWCU. He concludes that the use of legal literature adheres to the foundations and spirit of CRT, and there is a need to couple it with the storytelling and experiential knowledge tenet of CRT.[14] This would allow scholars to provide a more robust and complete picture of the exploitation of Black male athletes in the US educational system and at HWCU in particular.

Some scholars and commentators have embraced the notion that college athlete exploitation is a "myth," and that college athletes are actually privileged because they enjoy many benefits from their participation in big-time college sport at HWCU.[15] I acknowledged in chapter 1 that athletes do derive certain benefits from college sport participation, and the Black males interviewed for chapters 2 and 3 provide important examples of some of these tangible and intangible benefits. However, the argument that exploitation is a myth is overly simplistic and devoid of any real understanding of how race and other matters often negatively impact the education of Black male athletes. Derek Van Rheenen argues that exploitation occurs when one party receives unfair and undeserved benefits from its transactions or relationships with another. He acknowledges that economic exploitation (unfair financial compensation) exists to some degree in college sport, but focuses more specifically on the matter of academic exploitation. He sees the overrepresentation of Black male athletes on football and basketball teams and the corresponding lower graduation rates of this group in comparison to their peers as indicative of the racial and cultural divisions of opportunity. Moreover, he suggests that institutional racism has contributed to the exploitation of Black athletes and potentially other athletes in revenue-producing sports at HWCU.[16]

From a CRT perspective, the exploitation of Black athletes' labor in college sport is rooted in institutional racism. In chapter 2 Bobby, Mark, and Marcus all called out the hypocrisy and injustice of the NCAA's policies on athlete compensation. Given that Black male athletes represent the majority of football and basketball athletes at major Division I HWCU, such exploitation speaks to SRT's tenet of Whites' unjust enrichment and Blacks' unjust impoverishment. The salaries and other financial perks of Division I football coaches and athletics administrators, the majority of whom are White males, and restrictions on Black male athletes' financial benefits and opportunities beyond what the athletic scholarship allows go well beyond the economic benefits the former receive in comparison to the latter. The financial exchange is glaringly unfair when Black male athletes' labor produces more than the athletic scholarships they receive, and NCAA policies about amateurism prohibit athletes from capitalizing on their market value as other stakeholders are allowed to do. Even more importantly, exploitation also exists when HWCU promise educational opportunities to these athletes in exchange for their athletic services but the structural arrangements within these institutions are not conducive to HWCU holding up their end of the bargain. This education matter is one that Billy Hawkins specifically addresses in *The New Plantation*, and one that is also uncovered in the narratives of Black male athletes featured in this book.[17]

Meso-Level Matters

Organizational theory is generally concerned with the structure and design of organizations, and the causes and consequences of commonly occurring patterns in them. Sport management scholars have suggested there is a need to centralize issues of power and politics in the study of sport organizations by applying critical theory. Critical theory allows one to view organizations as operating in a wider cultural, economic, and political context characterized by historically entrenched asymmetrical power relations.[18] In *Understanding Sport Organizations*, sport management scholars Trevor Slack and Milena Parent discuss how we might categorize and better understand sport organizations and how they are managed. In particular, they draw from the work of Gareth Morgan to offer metaphors of organizations as cultures, organizations as political systems, and organizations as instruments of domination.[19] Slack and Parent do not explicitly embrace a critical race approach to examining sport organizations. However, I find CRT and SRT to be useful in further examining how racial privilege and disadvantage are distributed by and within the NCAA, athletic departments at HWCU, conference offices, and other college sport organizations that have profited greatly from the presence of Black male athletes. Therefore, my discussion of and elaboration on Slack and Parent's metaphors integrates critical, race-based perspectives.

The concept of organizations as cultures grew out of the idea that organizations are mini societies within larger societies. Organizational culture scholars are primarily concerned with understanding how shared values and meanings are created, maintained, and sometimes changed, particularly by leaders in organizations. Studying the organizational cultures of college athletic departments at HWCU can help scholars and practitioners understand how they shape the educational opportunities, experiences, and outcomes of Black male athletes. Eddie Comeaux and colleagues have discussed what they deem are the inherent contradictions between the cultures of universities and their athletic departments, and argue that athletes who come to play football and basketball at HWCU are often entering into a culture of low academic expectations and disengagement. In one study, they illuminate how the presence of state-of-the-art academic support centers, promotional materials, and other public statements promise a commitment to prioritizing academics and the "student" role but in reality, underlying messages and structures within the athletic department push athletes strongly toward athletics.[20] These messages are often communicated and reinforced by various organizational actors, from coaches to academic support personnel to the athletes themselves. During my work with Black male athletes in SUPER, one of the participants shared how the head football coach told him and his peers during a meeting their first day on campus that, "school and academics come first [as he held up two fingers], and football comes second [as he held up one finger]." This example speaks to the kinds of contradictory messages that Comeaux and colleagues stated are reinforced to athletes by coaches and other personnel.

As big-time college sport has continued to grow and HWCU have continued to recruit Black athletes, they have invested in state-of-the-art academic support centers and intensified the scope of services they offer. However, the role and effectiveness of these centers in addressing the unique needs of Black athletes has long been questioned, and it has been asserted that these centers might be "aiding and abetting a racial status-quo by emphasizing more of a social desire for sports entertainment."[21] The narratives I share in chapters 2 and 3 and my experiences as an academic mentor and college professor who has worked and interacted with academic support personnel across multiple HWCU reveals that some of them have (un)wittingly assisted in perpetuating racism and the status quo. The explicit or implicit pressures and demands that coaches and administrators often put on academic support personnel to keep athletes eligible to play is real, and these pressures can sometimes encourage personnel to engage in behaviors or practices that are detrimental to college athletes' educational opportunities, experiences, and outcomes. Academic scandals involving academic support staff in athletics (as well as faculty, coaches, and other stakeholder groups) at major universities over the years illustrate this reality.[22]

Scholars who view organizations as political systems are most interested in the power dynamics and discrepancies that exist between and among groups and individuals. In chapter 3, Marc lamented the "coach as savior" mentality and the unchecked power coaches often have over the athletes they recruit to HWCU. In chapter 2, Mark also expressed concerns about the inordinate amount of power and influence coaches have over the athletes they recruit and offer athletic scholarships to. Not only do coaches control athletes' playing time and the renewal of their athletic scholarships, but in some cases, may attempt to control athletes' social media presence or involvement in activities outside athletics, including membership in fraternities or other student organizations, or activism. In one notable example, Virginia Tech University men's head basketball coach, Buzz Williams, decided to "teach" his players (most of whom were Black) how to "respect" the national anthem. His players were told they had to at least memorize the words and "stand at attention" during the playing of the anthem before each game, and Williams even brought in military veterans to address the players about the importance of the national anthem.[23] Interestingly, Williams implemented this policy before Colin Kaepernick's controversial kneeling during the national anthem during the 2016 NFL season. I argue that such forced "patriotism" is not the hallmark of higher education, and is in fact antithetical to what higher education should be.

In thinking about organizations as instruments of domination from a critical perspective, organizations are entities designed to primarily benefit the interests of a privileged few (in this context, elite White males) at the expense of the masses. These organizations are often criticized for negatively exploiting their workers or labor force (college athletes), their host communities (local cities or towns HWCU are located in), and at times the environment to meet the ends and self-serving interests of the powerful elite. As discussed in the introduction and chapter 1, the NCAA and HWCU Division I athletic departments are highly political Eurocentric organizations that have been instruments of domination structured to privilege Whites, often at the expense of Black male athletes.[24] From a CRT perspective, these types of organizations embody the notion of Whiteness, but not just simply the idea that a socially and legally constructed racial category of people (i.e., Whites) are in control of the organizational hierarchy. More significantly, Whiteness is an ideology and system of assumptions and practices that undergird these organizations. From an SRT perspective, the White racial frame strongly influences how people think and comport themselves in these organizations.[25]

The academic capitalist model permeating the NCAA, conference offices, and the HWCU that are a part of these conferences and make up the NCAA's membership reflects this framing and the internal structures, processes, policies, and practices that flow from it. As mentioned throughout this book, most of the key decision makers in these organizations have been and continue to be White males who designed and implemented systems that disproportionately disadvantage Black athletes, particularly in the revenue-producing sports of football and men's basketball. The NCAA's much-talked-about and -criticized amateurism policy is a case in point:

> Student-athletes shall be amateurs in an intercollegiate sport, and their participation should be motivated primarily by education and by the physical, mental and social benefits to be derived. Student participation in intercollegiate athletics is an avocation, and student-athletes should be protected from exploitation by professional and commercial enterprises.[26]

Ironically, the claim that college athletes are amateurs who "should be protected from exploitation by professional and commercial enterprises" is completely contradicted by the exploitative nature of the academic capitalism model of governance. David Meggyesy, a White male who played college and professional football in the 1960s, puts it this way:

> The primary contradiction within the NCAA and, in particular, its top revenue producing schools is that, on one hand the amateur rules apply to the athletes and on the other, the rules of the market apply to the school's athletic department with the big exception being their labor costs. Putting it a different way, on one hand the NCAA and its member schools are non-profit educational entities, with their athlete employees categorized as student-athletes, and on the other their athletic departments, at the top level, are highly profitable commercial enterprises."[27]

This dominant institutional logic that amateurism defines the participants, but not the enterprise, is the epitome of hypocrisy and exploitation.

Sport management scholar Richard Southall, the founder and director of the College Sport Research Institute (CSRI), has for years been critical of the NCAA's notion of amateurism and the collegiate athletics model that has been created, disseminated, and imbedded in the institutional consciousness by the White NCAA presidents, conference commissioners, athletic directors, head football and men's basketball coaches who have run college sport.[28] Moreover, the academic capitalist position that there is no inherent conflict between commercial and educational logics (so as long as athletes are not engaging in commercial activity that directly benefits them) is used to justify the idea that engaging in big-time commercialized college sport is necessary to achieve educational opportunity for the vast majority of college athletes. In reality, however, the vast majority of athletes who benefit from these educational opportunities are White middle- to upper-class males and females who participate in the non-revenue sports that usually rely heavily on financial support from football and men's basketball (see quote by Victoria Jackson at the beginning of the introduction).

Although football and men's basketball are the most popular sports and generate the vast majority of interest and support from fans, the media, and corporate sponsors, some proponents of the academic capitalist model have argued that athletes' participation is not technically what generates revenue for athletic departments. Further, they argue that revenue sport athletes should not be treated any differently than their non-revenue peers because all athletes put in similar amounts of time and effort in their respective sports. I agree that athletes across all sports do put in hard work, but this framing is plagued by a woeful lack of understanding or outright denial of how race and racism contributes to the exploitative structural arrangements and management practices we see in college sport.

Micro-Level Matters

As Stanley Eitzen posits (see quotation above), when organizations exploit athletes for profit and then discard them without a meaningful education, it reinforces the stereotype that Black male athletes are physically superior but intellectually inferior. This White racial framing and stereotyping of Black male athletes as "dumb jocks" is something that was not lost on some of the Black males whose narratives I shared in this book. Since Harry Edwards's assertion that Black "dumb jocks" are not born but systematically created within American society and its educational and sport system, scholars have focused on how stereotyping affects the identity and educational experiences of Black male and female athletes.[29]

Some scholars have explicitly drawn from CRT to theorize about racial, social, economic, cultural, and psychological factors that impact Black athletes' academic and athletic experiences. For example, Samuel Hodge and colleagues focus on how Whites stereotype Black athletes as physically superior and intellectually inferior, and thus, steer them more toward athletic pursuits than academic ones. Moreover, they discuss how Black athletes sometimes buy into these negative stereotypes (i.e., they self-stereotype), and how internalizing these stereotypes negatively impacts their sense of self and motivation to achieve excellence beyond the domain of sport participation.[30] By limiting their identities to being athletes, Black males can exclude other important ways of seeing themselves, which contributes to their exploitation at HWCU.

Scholars have discussed the need to counter these stereotypes and called on coaches, faculty, administrators, academic support staff, and others (e.g., families, fans, sport media) to engage in thoughtful self-reflection into how their own personal race-sport stereotypic beliefs might influence their interactions with Black athletes. This is important because, as Hodge and colleagues have pointed out, psychological CRT "asserts that no one is exempt from the spontaneous and persistent influences of racism in America, thus self-reflection becomes a critical exercise for interaction with a diversity of student-athletes."[31] What this means is that we should not only be mindful of and address the destructive impact institutional racism might have on Black male athletes at HWCU, but we must better understand and address the internalized racism Black male athletes might wittingly or unwittingly perpetuate against and among themselves. In this regard, the most important stakeholder group to consider as we contemplate college sport reform and the educational rights of Black athletes are the athletes themselves and the role they ultimately play in combating the race-sport stereotypes. This is why I appreciate former NFL player Martellus Bennett's book, *Dear Black Boy*, which serves as a counter-narrative to the dominant narrative that Black males are only or best suited to be athletes. Bennett uses this book as a platform to push back against this racial stereotype, and to encourage young Black males to consider who they are and what else they have to offer the world beyond their athleticism.

As mentioned in the introduction, Harry Edwards has argued for decades that education is an activist pursuit that Black athletes must take a substantial role in prioritizing and attaining. From a CRT perspective, this educational activism involves Black athletes working with relevant stakeholders across racial groups to ensure they receive a balanced, well-rounded educational experience. Furthermore, it also entails Black athletes' active resistance against some of the historical, social, cultural, structural, political, economic, and psychological forces at play in American society and the Eurocentric organizations that make up the athletics industrial complex. To varying degrees, the Black male athletes who participated in my study did indeed view education as an activist pursuit. Recall John's powerful narrative from chapter 3, where he shared how dealing with the injuries he endured during his college playing career forced him to come to grips with who he was without a ball in his hand and to take an active role in pursuing meaningful identities beyond the playing field.

As the above discussion suggests, we need to view Black male athletes' education matters as multilevel, where the focus should be centered on how the elite White male dominance in US society, its educational system, and college sport is foundational to our understanding of educational challenges Black male athletes face. The prevalence of racial stereotyping on the macro, meso, and micro level must be an important part of the discourse and action related to college sport reform as well.

IMPLICATIONS FOR RESEARCH, POLICY, AND PRACTICE
Research Considerations

Literature on the intersection of race, sports and education offers a number of research directions worth continuing or further exploring. First and foremost, we should continue hearing and documenting the stories and perspectives of Black male athletes in both higher and secondary education. This means giving these athletes' a seat at the table and centralizing their voices and experiential knowledge in discourse on college sport reform. We should celebrate Black male athletes "as critical theorists" who are arguably best positioned to bring valuable insight and knowledge to this conversation about reform both within the academic literature and in discussions on policy and practice among leaders and practitioners in higher education and college sport.[32] In this regard, scholars should consider engaging in several different modes of inquiry to advance important practical and emancipatory knowledge that is rooted in the lived experiences and voices of Black male athletes and their peers; case studies, narrative inquiry, participatory action research, ethnography, grounded theory, and phenomenology are all examples of different, yet complimentary, approaches to the study of and with Black male athletes. These approaches invite Black male athletes to become co-creators of knowledge about themselves, and scholars to secure and present powerful stories about Black male athletes' education.

Second, in the spirit of CRT, scholars should not only analyze legal cases involving the educational and other rights of Black male college athletes, but they should also consider interrogating the policies, rules, and other documents that pertain to the structures, functions, and activities in college sport. In this regard, the NCAA rules manual and related documents should become the subject of study. In addition, the mission statements and other documents and programs within athletic departments should be analyzed and critiqued. Some scholars have already critically explored the mission statements, department philosophies and other organizational directives of athletic departments at HWCU and uncovered how racial inequities are maintained in systemic and institutionalized ways in these spaces.[33] Extended examinations of such directives could further expose and provide better understanding on how institutional racism is an education matter.

Third, scholars should further investigate the role of historically Black colleges and universities (HBCU) in the education of Black male athletes. Joseph Cooper and colleagues have conducted some important research that examines educational experiences of Black males and females in this educational context.[34] I believe there is a need for continued research with and about Black athletes in these settings. Scholars should continue this work via case studies on individual athletes, teams, and/or athletic departments at HBCU to learn more about various education matters in these spaces. Moreover, they should continue to compare the experiences and outcomes of Black athletes at HBCU and HWCU and critically examine why some Black athletes might chose HBCU over HWCU. I have observed, at least anecdotally, what appears to be the beginning of a pattern where more and more highly recruited Black male high school football athletes are choosing to attend HBCU instead of the FBS Division I programs at HWCU. Indeed, given that these HWCU have consistently cherry-picked and monopolized the athletic talent of Black male athletes since the early 1970s, it would be fascinating to learn more about why some Black male athletes are taking their gifts and talents back to HBCU.

Finally, scholars and practitioners should also conduct large-scale quantitative survey studies that assess Black male athletes' and their peers' perceptions and attitudes about their educational opportunities, experiences, and outcomes stemming from their participation in organized school sport in both secondary and postsecondary institutions. Such technical knowledge would also tell a story and provide important insight into the thinking of these athletes. Large data sets have been collected on this topic in the past, but there is a need for more of these types of studies from groups and individuals—both within and outside the US educational and college sport systems.[35]

Policy and Practical Considerations for Leaders and Practitioners in Higher Education and College Sport

In 2009, Allen Sack identified the major issues and assumptions that divide reformers and reform groups. More specifically, he discussed three different conceptual models—intellectual elitist, academic capitalist, and athletes' rights—to interpret the reality of commercialized college sport. The biggest differences between these models has been the assumptions each makes about the relationship between commercialism and academic values, the educational impact and legal status of athletic scholarships, and the mission of higher education.

As I have discussed throughout this book, academic capitalism has been the predominant governance model for the NCAA and its member institutions. Critics of this model have typically adopted the intellectual elitist and/or athletes' rights models, both of which have focused on addressing the economic and academic exploitation of college athletes. The intellectual elitist model has been highly critical of athletic commercialism and the subsidization of athletes in the form of athletic scholarships. Some examples of reforms promoted by this camp include:

- The replacement of one-year, renewable athletic scholarships with need-based aid or scholarships whose renewal is not dependent on athletic performance
- The restoration of freshman ineligibility, particularly for "special admits"[36]
- Ensuring that athletes can pursue their major of choice, and that athletic contests do not interfere with class attendance
- Making the location and control of academic support services for athletes the same as that for all students at the university
- Requiring athletes to fit the same academic profile as all other students
- Requiring that athletes maintain a cumulative GPA of 2.0 each semester to be eligible
- Supplying full disclosure of aggregate data on the majors, advisers, GPA, courses taken, and names of instructors for all athletes
- Closely monitoring the growth rate of operating expenditures in sport programs

Proponents of the athletes' rights model acknowledge that college sport as commercial entertainment is deeply and likely permanently embedded in American life and higher education. They argue that athletes are not only students, but also workers who deserve to benefit from free enterprise and the fruits of their labor. Some of the most popular reform measures proposed by this camp include:

- Legislative initiatives to secure worker's compensation rights for college athletes
- Organizing college athletes and forming alliances with organized labor
- Challenging the NCAA on antitrust grounds to increase financial support and other benefits (e.g., medical) for athletes
- Filling lawsuits against the NCAA to allow athletes to secure sponsorships and other benefits related to their image and likeness

Outgrowths of the athletes' rights model include the attempts of Northwestern University's players to unionize and various lawsuits brought against the NCAA by college athletes that, for example, challenge rules and policies related to the use of college athletes' likenesses for commercial purposes, challenge lifestyle restrictions placed on athletes, and challenge disparities between athletes' grants and aids and cost of attendance.[37] Such efforts have certainly put pressure on the NCAA to reconsider its unjust policies related to amateurism. As I was finishing this book, the NCAA had begun considering if it should allow athletes to profit from their name.

From a CRT and SRT perspective, the foci of these reform models and the recent developments that have emerged from them are a step in the right direction toward addressing the economic and academic exploitation of Black athletes and all athletes more generally. However, I would argue there is a need to go further in centralizing and explicitly focusing on race and racism. For example, Billy Hawkins's focus on decolonization, reform, and the Black athlete in *The New Plantation* is most closely aligned with a CRT and SRT approach to college sport reform, particularly because of its explicit emancipatory focus. While he acknowledges that many of the reformers and reform groups are well-meaning, competent individuals and leaders, he criticizes some of the reform demands and recommendations of the intellectual elitist (e.g., admissions recommendations) and academic capitalist (e.g., Academic Progress Rate [APR] standards) camps, suggesting they are designed to "ethnically cleanse and re-Whiten" college football and basketball. In describing Black athletes in football and basketball at HWCU as internally colonized individuals, Hawkins grounds his reform recommendations within the process of decolonization, which he describes as an emancipatory strategy that moves beyond an appeal to a moral adjustment to "a fundamental change in structural arrangements and the distribution of resources, and an access to services previously denied."[38] Although he does not necessarily view the issue of academic integrity and college sport reform as solely a "Black athlete problem," he does acknowledge that Black athletes are disproportionately affected by the "archaic racial ideologies" from which these Eurocentric organizations operate.

Hawkins's recommendations focus on addressing reform in the communities and school systems these athletes are recruited from by these HWCU. He suggests that these organizations need to invest in the academic development of Black male athletes by helping to build the academic infrastructures of their communities and schools. Doing so will help create students who are better academically prepared for higher education, and empowered to face the academic challenges once they arrive on campus. This investment in building up communities' academic infrastructures would be one systemic and powerful way to help address educational pipeline matters we see with some Black male athletes who transition from P–12 into higher education. Other reforms recommended by Hawkins relate to the academic progress of athletes, including allowing college athletes to take a lighter course load (e.g., 6–9 hours); this reform would increase opportunities for Black male athletes to learn and perform well academically, while also being able to fully explore a meaningful major and degree path.

Hawkins argues for a greater distribution of resources to the athletes, even if that means redirecting some financial perks from coaches to the athletes. I concur wholeheartedly with this suggestion, especially given the outrageously high dollar values (and related perks) in college football and basketball coaching contracts today. Hawkins also discusses the contractual nature of the relationship between these athletes and organizations, and suggests these organizations create incentives that encourage elite athletes to invest more time in college and support systems that provide benefits to the vast majority who do not make it to the professional level after they graduate. Such benefits include financial support for graduate school, medical benefits for life in the event of life-altering injury, career counseling support, and emeritus status, among others. In concluding his discussion of reform, Hawkins provides a summary overview and highlights additional reforms rooted in decolonization:

- Focus on Black athlete self-empowerment and understand and negotiate rights as a student and athlete.

- Decrease commercialism and exploitation or increase funding for athletes.
- Diversify leadership structure and incorporate voice of Black athlete in the political/governing process.
- Increase racial and cultural diversity throughout university structure.

Many of the recommendations of the Black males in chapters 2 and 3 align with those laid out by Hawkins.

Kenneth Shropshire and Collin Williams more recently presented equity-focused, athlete-centered ideas for ways we might fix college sports. Although these authors are not as explicit as Hawkins in discussing race and racism, they argue that being equity-minded requires leaders and practitioners in college sport to move away from a one-size-fits-all mentality and instead take individual athletes as they are and allow them to enter into a system that offers a path to success that will work for them. The authors present a student-athlete manifesto that focuses on customizing a process that graduates and focuses on future employment and life opportunities for all college athletes, but particularly those who are from low-income, first-generation, and racial minority backgrounds. This manifesto, which includes some of the suggestions and recommendations from Hawkins and the Black male athletes featured in chapter 2 and 3, outlines several steps to success for all athletes by accounting for these most vulnerable groups:

- Make obtaining a meaningful degree the top priority.
- Broaden the pathway to meaningful degree completion (lifetime scholarships).
- Mandate academic boot camps for entering student-athletes and professional boot camps for exiting student-athletes.
- Make maximum use of summers for educational and professional development.
- Expand the opportunity to get credits from institutions offering online courses.
- Provide personalized counseling on the best academic and career paths.
- Review and enforce existing limits on hours of sports participation.
- Enhance tutoring support.
- Ensure that athletes are actually the ones doing the academic work.

- More stringently prohibit athlete-only or athlete-dominant courses (i.e., clustering).
- Standardize a way to more accurately track all graduation rates.
- Establish independently administered pre- and post-tests to truly measure learning.
- Increase accountability by requiring the NCAA to routinely report this data disaggregated by race, sex, sport, division, and particular subsets of institutions within a division.[39]

In reflecting on the utility of Shropshire and Williams's proposed reforms directed specifically at Black male college athletes, it is important to note that many of these individuals come to these HWCU with what CRT and education scholar Tara Yosso terms *community cultural wealth*. This includes an array of cultural knowledge, skills, abilities, contacts, and other assets that racial minorities possess, but that often go unacknowledged in educational spaces where Whiteness is the norm or standard. Yosso identified six forms of capital that should be viewed not as cultural deficits, but as strengths racial minority students bring with them to these spaces: aspirational, linguistic, familial, social, resistant, and navigational.[40] Black male athletes possess these and other forms of capital that extend beyond their athletic gifts and talents. Leaders and practitioners at HWCU must be intentional about recognizing and using this capital to help these athletes reach their full potential as students at these institutions. This equity-centered mind-set is in alignment with the Universal Design for Learning (UDL) framework, which posits that because each learner is unique, educators should proactively and deliberately design curriculum and learning environments, activities, and opportunities in ways that support the success of each student.[41] In this regard, principles of UDL have relevance to the educational plight of Black male athletes and their peers at HWCU and should be a part of the conversation on college sport reform.

Race-based reform measures align well with CRT and SRT because they focus on addressing what is "wrong" with the structures, processes, and policies in these Eurocentric organizations, instead of viewing Black athletes as the problem. In *Race Matters*, CRT proponent Cornel West argued that when discussing and addressing issues of race and racism in America it is important that we begin not with the "problems of black people" but with "flaws of American society—flaws rooted in the historic inequalities and longstanding cultural stereotypes."[42] Such should be the case when we consider Black athletes' history and ongoing journey in the American educational system and big-time college sport. Black athletes in the twenty-first century might not face the same blatant forms of racism their predecessors had to endure (even though in this Trump era, such overt racism has been making a comeback). Nonetheless, the covert, systemic racism today's Black athletes face is no less virulent and is arguably more destructive in the long term. An examination of the educational plight of Black athletes through a CRT and SRT lens provides additional insight into the flaws in American society and its social institutions, and gives us clear directives for research, policy, and practice related to college sport going forward.

Athletic departments at HWCU should upgrade and improve their academic support and other programs by supporting and/or implementing programs designed to address the challenges and needs of Black athletes at HWCU. These programs could be housed both within and outside the jurisdiction of the NCAA and its member institutions. Initiatives such as the Collective Uplift program, which was founded in 2014 at the University of Connecticut "to educate, empower, nurture, and support students across ethnic backgrounds to maximize their holistic potential both within and beyond athletic contexts," is a great example.[43] The core tenets include holistic development, cultural empowerment, community outreach, and positive campus experiences. This program, which was co-constructed or co-created by the students and their faculty adviser, comprises weekly sessions year-round and is operated without the oversight of the athletic department. More such culturally relevant programs are needed on the campuses of these HWCU.

Related to these points above, scholars and other social commentators, including some of the Black male athletes featured in this book, have called for more diversity in the leadership structure of these HWCU and their athletic departments. More specifically, as Joseph Cooper and his colleagues have argued, there is a need for more culturally responsive and race-conscious leadership in these college sport programs and their host institutions.[44] It is not enough to hire a Black person or person of color into these leadership roles; if that leader is unable or unwilling to acknowledge the role of race when it comes to understanding and addressing Black male athletes' education matters, it could actually be counterproductive. In this regard, there is a need for those elite White males who continue to over-see college sport at HWCU and their acolytes who manage the day-to-day affairs and operations in these organizations to acknowledge that race matters and to hire and promote individuals from diverse backgrounds who understand this reality.

Given their intimate relationship with athletes and the critical role they play in the educational opportunities, experiences and outcomes of athletes, head coaches and their staffs should be willing to embrace and support academic support programs and initiatives such as the ones described above. While there are of course some coaches who do support such programs and initiatives and have a genuine interest in the educational experiences and outcomes of their athletes, there are many others who appear to be more concerned with serving their own interest (signing the next top recruiting class, securing a lucrative contract, winning games, etc.). In this regard, as Marc suggested in chapter 3, mechanisms for holding coaches accountable for how they go about addressing the educational interests of Black male and other athletes need to be implemented. Because their primary purpose is to foster the growth and development of racial minorities at various levels of sport, organizations such as the Black Coaches and Administrators (BCA) should be involved in this process. The BCA and similar bodies should partner with other organizations in creating mandates to challenge their own membership and coaching professionals throughout the NCAA to focus not only on the athletic development of their athletes, but also the social and intellectual aspects of athlete development.

Black male college athletes must also be involved in the process and take charge of their educational interests by aligning themselves with programs, coalitions, alliances, and people who will enlighten and support them during their time on campus. As their interviews from chapter 3 show, this is something John and Willis were able to do, especially once injury prematurely ended their college playing careers. It is imperative that Black male athletes assess and evaluate their priorities and preferences by focusing on why they are on campus and what benefits beyond participating in sport they can take away from their experiences. To be sure, in a few cases, the most talented athletes view their time on these HWCU campuses (sometimes only one to three years) merely as a stepping-stone to the NBA or NFL. But even in those cases, it could behoove them to find ways to benefit from the vast resources offered on these campuses. For example,

I remember how at the 2018 Black Student-Athlete Summit, University of Texas men's head basketball coach Shaka Smart shared that he worked with their academic support staff to help one of his "one and done" Black athletes (he was entering the NBA draft after his freshman year) chose a class schedule during his first and only semester on campus that could help prepare him for success in life and his professional playing career going forward. In particular, they encouraged him to take a personal finance class to learn how to handle becoming and being a millionaire, and a Black history class to learn more about his history while also connecting with Black faculty mentors who taught the class and had a history of working with Black male athletes. This is a great example of a Black male athlete who was able to maximize his educational experiences for the short time he was on campus. Some of the Black male athletes featured in this book spoke to the importance of tapping into the vast resources available on these campuses, whether they be people, courses, programs and events, or organizations and activities beyond what the athletic department had to offer.

Policy and Practical Considerations for Leaders and Practitioners in Secondary Education and High School Sport

Black male athletes in the P–12 educational context and the educational stakeholders who help prepare them for higher education play an important role in addressing many of the education matters mentioned throughout this book. In particular, coaches, teachers, and academic guidance counselors are critical in helping address educational pipeline matters. Given the powerful sphere of influence coaches often have on their athletes, they are arguably in the best position to influence their educational ambitions. The movie *Coach Carter*, which is based on a true story of a high school basketball coach, is a great example of the positive and powerful effect that coaches could have on their athletes' identities and educational development.[45] In the movie, actor Samuel L. Jackson plays Coach Ken Carter, a Black male who uses "tough love" tactics to win over and convince his mostly Black male athletes that life is much bigger and more than the game of basketball. In light of the fact that coaches typically have the most direct and immediate influence on the interscholastic sport experiences of their athletes, I offer the following recommendations to coaches:

- Consult with athletes, parents/guardians, administrators, teachers, counselors, and researchers to determine the educational needs of athletes and develop programming to meet those needs.
- Join social justice organizations such as the BCA and take advantage of professional development opportunities made available via these organizations.
- Bring in former athletes who pursued various paths after high school, including those who pursued college and professional sport playing careers as well as those who did not.
- Embrace programs such as the "Scholar-Baller" program, which was designed by C. Keith Harrison and colleagues to challenge athletes to harmonize their academic and athletic identities.

Because they have the most direct and immediate influence on the academic experiences of Black male athletes, teachers serve perhaps the most important function in preparing these athletes for higher education. Research has revealed that high school teachers, the majority of whom tend to be White females, often stereotype Black male athletes as "dumb jocks," but also give them unearned grades and other preferential treatment because of their athlete status at the schools.[46] My observations and conversations over the years with Black male athletes who were blue-chip prospects in high school provides support for these research findings. Unfortunately, this treatment of Black male athletes often denies them the opportunity to demonstrate their academic abilities to their teachers. Therefore, I offer the following recommendations for teachers:

- Recognize the unique challenges that Black male athletes might face, but pay attention to how both cognitive/intellectual and non-cognitive/motivation factors influence Black male athletes' academic interests, development, and performance.
- Make concerted efforts to learn more about Black male athletes' lived realities and contexts outside the school. This might include attending their sporting events and other team-related functions and carving out time and space to engage Black male athletes in dialogue about their learning interests and needs.

- Familiarize themselves with the linguistic capital of Black male students, both athletes and non-athletes, and when appropriate, incorporate it into lesson plans. For example, the influence of hip-hop in the Black community is important to acknowledge and use as a tool to assist in the learning process. Teachers should also strategically utilize and leverage social media and technology to engage Black male athletes and their peers in the learning environment.
- Engage in professional development opportunities geared toward serving students from diverse backgrounds. For example, organizations such as the American Educational Research Association has a special-interest group that focuses on research and issues related to education and sport, and the University of Texas at Austin has hosted the Black Student-Athlete Summit each year since 2015.
- Related to all the points above, teachers should learn about the UDL framework, and gradually implement UDL principles into their classrooms and other educational spaces.

Finally, academic guidance counselors are also important educational stakeholders who are in a position to help prepare Black male athletes for higher education opportunities. During my initial years as a faculty member at James Madison University, I served in a diversity recruitment program sponsored by the university president's office that placed faculty from the university in urban and rural high schools throughout the state. During my weekly visits to the school, I worked directly with academic counselors, among other groups, to help prepare students in general (some happened to be athletes) for opportunities in higher education. I learned that their primary responsibilities involved helping students learn about certain academic requirements they needed to fulfill to graduate from high school and be eligible for higher education and other opportunities. But they also have a responsibility to assist students with career awareness and planning. This could be an invaluable service that counselors provide for Black males who are being recruited to play college sport. In this regard, I offer the following recommendations to academic counselors:

- Meet regularly with Black male athletes beginning with their first year in secondary education, and begin establishing trust and rapport with them.

- Help them establish a plan that includes specific, measurable, alterable, realistic and time-based academic and career goals throughout their years in school. This involves exploring their strengths and assets, likes and dislikes, and resources to help in the transition into higher education and college sport.
- Become familiar with and and share the NCAA's and other sport-governing bodies' guidelines for eligibility, including GPA and standardized test scores, with these Black males early on in their schooling. This also should include working with coaches, teachers, and administrators to communicate this information to these students.
- Identify college preparatory programs and urge Black male athletes to participate in them early and often.
- Work with other educational stakeholders to create programs and workshops that allow Black male athletes to explore and gain valuable career and work experiences such as internships and practicums, career fairs, and volunteering.

CONCLUDING THOUGHTS

In this book, I drew from my background and lived experiences working with Black male college athletes at HWCU to illuminate pertinent matters that influence educational opportunities, experiences, and outcomes for this historically underserved and disenfranchised student population. The narratives of the Black male college athletes in chapters 2 and 3 identified notable challenges they faced in the pipeline from P–12 schooling into higher education, but more importantly, how they successfully navigated the world of college sport in this era of academic capitalism in higher education. The powerful stories and perspectives of the twelve Black male college athletes who are highlighted in *Race, Sports, and Education* are in many ways important counter-narratives to the rhetoric of the academic capitalist model of college sport reform. It is my hope that the voices of these Black males are informative and inspirational for current and future Black male college athletes who give so much to the historically White colleges and universities they attend.

Notes

Series Foreword

1. D. Bell, "Racial Realism," *Connecticut Law Review* 24, no. 2 (1991): 363–379.
2. Y. J. Majors, *Shoptalk: Lessons in Teaching from an African American Hair Salon* (New York: Teachers College Press, 2015).
3. P. Freire, *Pedagogy of the Oppressed* (New York: Bloomsbury Publishing, 2018).

Introduction

1. V. L. Jackson, "Take It From a Former Division I Athlete: College Sports Are Like Jim Crow," *Los Angeles Times*, January 11, 2018.
2. E. Sermon, "Do You Know," *Chilltown, New York* (New York: Universal Motown Records, 2004), CD.
3. H. Edwards, "Transformational Developments at the Interface of Race, Sport, and the Collegiate Athletic Arms Race in the Age of Globalization," *Journal of Intercollegiate Sport* 4 (2011): 18–31.
4. According to the 1997 HBO documentary *The Journey of the African American Athlete*, it was the dominant performance by a Black running back for the University of Southern California named Sam "Bam" Cunningham in a victory against the legendary coach, Paul "Bear" Bryant's all-White Alabama squad in 1970 that really prompted these HWCU to begin regularly recruiting and offering Black male athletes scholarships. See L. D. Farrell et al., *The Journey of the African American Athlete* (New York: HBO Studio & Broadcast Operations, 1996).
5. H. Edwards, *The Revolt of the Black Athlete* (New York: Free Press, 1969); H. Edwards, *Sociology of Sport* (Homewood, IL: Dorsey 1973); F. G. Polite and B. Hawkins, eds., *Sport, Race, Activism, and Social Change: The Impact of Dr. Harry Edwards' Scholarship and Service* (San Diego, CA: Cognella, 2012).
6. E. Smith, *Race, Sport and the American Dream* (Durham, NC: Carolina Academic Press, 2007), 121.
7. B. Hawkins, *The New Plantation: Black Athletes, College Sports, and Predominantly White NCAA Institutions* (New York: Palgrave MacMillan, 2010).
8. R. A. Bennett III et al., eds., *Black Males and Intercollegiate Athletics: An Exploration of Problems and Solutions* (Bradford, UK: Emerald, 2015).

9. J. N. Cooper, *From Exploitation Back to Empowerment: Black Male Holistic (Under)Development Through Sport and (Mis)Education* (New York: Peter Lang, 2019).

10. T. E. Dancy II, K. T. Edwards, and J. E. Davis, "Historically White Universities and Plantation Politics: Anti-Blackness and Higher Education in the Black Lives Matter Era," *Urban Education* 53, no. 2 (2018): 176–195.

11. S. R. Harper, *Black Male Student-Athletes and Racial Inequities in NCAA Division I Revenue Generating College Sports* (Philadelphia: University of Pennsylvania, Center for the Study of Race and Equity in Education, 2016).

12. F. A. Bonner II, "Introduction: Strengthening the Pipeline: A Need for Frameworks and Models in Black Male Research," in *Building on Resilience: Models and Frameworks of Black Male Success Across the P–20 Pipeline*, ed. F. A. Bonner II (Sterling, VA: Stylus, 2014): 1–9.

13. H. Edwards, "The Black 'Dumb Jock': An American Sports Tragedy," *College Board Review* 131 (1984): 8–13.

14. The focus is on Division I programs at HWCU because they are typically the most competitive, with highly skilled athletes, and have the largest operating budgets, commercial appeal, and visibility on the national (in some cases, international) and regional stage. Included in this group are the so-called mid-major Division I programs (typically regional in terms of visibility and commercial appeal) because although they do not necessarily have the same caliber athletes, operating budgets, visibility, and commercial appeal as the higher-profile major programs, athletes in these programs are still talented and often face similar educational challenges. My focus on Division I athletes is not to suggest that Division II and III, NAIA, and junior college athletes are unimportant; although these athletes might not face some of the challenges their Division I counterparts face, they still have an important story to tell as participants in sport at the college level.

15. These could be oral and/or written reflections and accounts of Black male athletes' past and/or present experiences in education and sport.

16. J. N. Cooper, "Excellence Beyond Athletics: Best Practices for Enhancing Black Male Student Athletes' Educational Experiences and Outcomes," *Equity & Excellence in Education* 49, no. 3 (2016): 267–283.

17. Edwards, "The Black 'Dumb Jock.'"

18. H. Edwards, "The Promise and Limits of Leveraging Black Athlete Power to Compel Campus Change," *Journal of Higher Education Athletics & Innovation* 1, no.1 (2016): 4–13.

19. H. Edwards, "Paradigm Shift: Partnering in Elevating the Status, Circumstances and Outcomes of Women and Girls," The Dr. Harry Edwards Lectures, University of Texas, Austin, Texas, April 7–9, 2015.

20. J. E. Bruening, "Gender and Racial Analysis: Are All the Women White, and All the Blacks Men?" *Quest* 57 (2005): 330–349.

21. A. R. Carter-Francique, D. Dortch, and K. Carter-Phiri, "Black Female College Athletes' Perceptions of Power in Sport And Society," *Journal for the Study of Sports and Athletes in Education* 11, no. 1 (2017): 18–45; A. R. Carter-Francique, "Black Female Collegiate Athlete Experiences in a Culturally Relevant Leadership Program," *National Journal of Urban Education & Practice* 7, no. 2 (2013): 87–106; A. R. Carter and A. Hart, " Perspectives of Mentoring: The Black Female Student-Athlete," *Sport Management Review* 13 (2010): 382–394.

22. F. L. Uperesa, "Addressing Hyper/In-Visibility: A Roundtable on Preliminary Research with Pacific Islander Student-Athletes," *Amerasia Journal* 41, no. 2 (2015): 69–85.

23. T. Shakur, rec. as Makaveli, "White Man'z World," *The Don Killuminati: The 7 Day Theory* (Los Angeles: Death Row Records and Interscope, 1996), CD; J. Feagin and K. Ducey, *Elite White Men Ruling: Who, What, When, Where, and How* (New York: Routledge, 2017).

24. The elite White male dominance system is heavily rooted in sociologist Joe Feagin's conceptualization of *systemic racism theory*. According to Feagin, "systemic racism encompasses a broad range of racialized dimensions of this society: the racist framing, racist ideology, stereotyped attitudes, racist emotions, discriminatory habits and actions, and extensive racist institutions developed over centuries by whites"; see J. R. Feagin, *Systemic Racism: A Theory of Oppression* (New York: Routledge, 2006), xii.

25. R. A. Smith, *Sports and Freedom: The Rise of Big-Time College Athletics* (New York: Oxford University Press, 1988).

26. A. J. Weems and J. N. Singer, "Racial Barriers In Eurocentric Sport(ing) Institutions: Countering the White Racial Frame," in *Systemic Racism: Making Liberty, Justice, and Democracy Real*, ed. R. Thompson-Miller and K. Ducey (New York: Palgrave-Macmillan, 2017), 285–306.

27. A. Zimbalist, *Unpaid Professionals: Commercialism and Conflict in Big-Time College Sports* (Princeton, NJ: Princeton University Press, 1999).

28. W. Byers and C. Hammer, *Unsportsmanlike Conduct: Exploiting College Athletes* (Ann Arbor: University of Michigan Press, 1995).

29. J. Nocera, "The Man Who Built the NCAA," *New York Times*, May 29, 2015.

30. D. Stovall, "Forging Community in Race and Class: Critical Race Theory and the Quest for Social Justice in Education," *Race, Ethnicity, and Education* 9 (2006): 243–259.

31. T. Curry, *The Man-Not: Race, Class, Genre, and the Dilemmas of Black Manhood.* (Philadelphia: Temple University Press, 2017), 4.

Chapter 1

1. W. Watkins, *The White Architects of Black Education: Ideology and Power in America, 1865–1954* (New York: Teachers College Press, 2001).

2. C. G. Woodson, *The Education of the Negro* (Brooklyn, NY: A&B Publishers Group, 1998).

3. B. Hawkins, *The New Plantation: Black Athletes, College Sports, and Predominantly White NCAA Institutions* (New York: Palgrave MacMillan, 2010).

4. H. R. Milner, "Race, Culture, and Researcher Positionality: Working Through Dangers Seen, Unseen, and Unforeseen," *Educational Researcher* 36, no. 7 (2007): 388–400.

5. C. West, *Race Matters* (New York: Vintage Books, 1994).

6. G. Ladson-Billings and W. Tate, "Toward a Critical Race Theory of Education," *Teachers College Record* 97 (1995): 47–68; W. F. Tate, "Critical Race Theory in Education: History, Theory, and Implications," *Review of Research in Education* 22 (1997): 195–247; G. Ladson-Billings, "Just What Is Critical Race Theory and What's It Doing in a *Nice* Field Like Education?" *International Journal of Qualitative Studies in Education* 11, no. 1 (1998): 7–24.

7. M. Lynn and A. D. Dixson, eds., *Handbook of Critical Race Theory in Education* (New York: Routledge, 2013).

8. T. C. Howard, *Black Male(d): Peril and Promise in the Education of African American Males* (New York: Teachers College Press, 2014).

9. J. N. Singer, "The Mis-education of African American Male College Athletes," in *Introduction to Intercollegiate Athletics*, ed. E. Comeaux (Baltimore: Johns Hopkins University Press, 2015), 193–206.

10. See C. Royal and M. L. Hill, "Fight the Power: Making #BlackLivesMatter in Urban Education: Introduction to the Special Issue," *Urban Education* 53, no. 2 (2018):143–144; K. Y. Taylor, *From #BlackLivesMatter to Black Liberation* (Chicago: Haymarket Books, 2016).

11. Although Obama is biracial (his father is an African man from Kenya and his mother is a White woman from Kansas), by social norms he is considered Black. Moreover, Obama identified himself as Black in his book; see B. Obama, *The Audacity of Hope: Thoughts on Reclaiming the American Dream* (New York: Crown Publishers, 2006).

12. W. J. Wilson, *The Declining Significance of Race: Blacks and Changing American Institutions* (Chicago: University of Chicago Press, 1978); D. D'Souza, *The End of Racism* (New York: Free Press Paperbacks, 1995).

13. C. West, *Real Time with Bill Maher*, Season 15, Episode 16, May 19, 2017, Home Box Office.

14. H. Edwards, "The Promise and Limits of Leveraging Black Athlete Power Potential to Compel Campus Change," *Journal of Higher Education Athletics & Innovation* 1, no. 1 (2016): 4–13.

15. M. Bennett and D. Zirin, *Things That Make White People Uncomfortable* (Chicago: Haymarket Books, 2018).

16. E. Thomas, *We Matter: Athletes and Activism* (Brooklyn, NY: Akashic Books, 2018), 296.

17. Athletes' rights advocates view college sport as a commercial enterprise that will remain deeply embedded in the fabric of American life, and thus athletes, like all other stakeholders, should have certain rights and protections in such a system; see A. Sack, "Clashing Models of Commercial Sport in Higher Education: Implications for Reform and Scholarly Research," *Journal of Issues in Intercollegiate Athletics* 2 (2009): 76–92.

18. J. H. Clarke, *Africans at the Crossroads: Notes for an African World Revolution* (Trenton, NJ: Africa World Press, 1991).

19. J. Gaston-Gayles, A. Bryant Rockenbach, and H. A. Davis, "Civic Responsibility and the Student Athlete: Validating a New Conceptual Model," *Journal of Higher Education* 83, no. 4 (2012): 535–557.

20. A. D. Dixson and C. K. Rousseau, "And We Are Still Not Saved: Critical Race Theory in Education Ten Years Later," *Race, Ethnicity and Education* 8, no. 1 (2005): 7–27.

21. E. O. Hutchinson, *The Assassination of the Black Male Image* (New York: Touchstone, 1996).

22. J. L. White and J. H. Cones III, *Black Man Emerging: Facing the Past and Seizing a Future in America* (New York: Routledge, 1999).

23. E. Cose, *The Envy of the World: On Being a Black Man in America* (New York: Washington Square Press, 2002).

24. T. J. Curry, *The Man-Not: Race, Class, Genre, and the Dilemmas of Black Manhood* (Philadelphia: Temple University Press, 2017), 29.

25. W. Muhammad, *Understanding the Assault on the Black Man, Black Manhood, and Black Masculinity* (Atlanta: A-Team Publishing, 2016).

26. L. Harrison Jr., C. K. Harrison, and L. N. Moore, "African American Racial Identity and Sport. *Sport, Education, and Society* 7, no. 2 (2002): 122–133.

27. Howard, *Black Male(d)*.

28. D. Bell, "Brown vs. Board of Education and the Interest-Convergence Principle," *Harvard Law Review* 93 (1980): 518–533.

29. J. Donner," Towards an Interest-Convergence in the Education of African-American Football Student Athletes in Major College Sports," *Race, Ethnicity and Education* 8, no. 1 (2005): 45–67.

30. S. Harper, *Black Male Student-Athletes and Racial Inequities in Division-I Revenue-Generating College Sports* (Philadelphia: University of Pennsylvania, Center for the Study of Race and Equity in Education, 2016).

31. D. S. Eitzen, *Fair or Foul: Beyond the Myths and Paradoxes of Sport*, 2nd ed. (Lanham, MD: Rowman & Littlefield, 2003), 111.

32. C.K. Harrison, E. Comeaux, and M. Plecha, "Faculty and Male Football and Basketball Players on University Campuses: An Empirical Investigation of the "Intellectual" as Mentor to the Student Athlete," *Research Quarterly for Exercise and Sport* 77, no. 2 (2006): 277–284.

33. D.A. Houston and L.D. Baber, "Academic Clustering Among Football

Student-Athletes and Exploring Its Relationship to Institutional Character-istics," *Journal for the Study of Sports and Athletes in Education* 11, no. 1 (2017): 66–90.

34. P. A. Adler and P. Adler, *Backboards and Blackboards: College Athletes and Role Engulfment* (New York: Columbia University Press, 1991).

35. R. King-White, ed., *Sport and the Neoliberal University: Profit, Politics, and Pedagogy* (New Brunswick, NJ: Rutgers University Press, 2018).

36. P. A. Noguera, *The Trouble with Black Boys . . . and Other Reflections on Race, Equity, and the Future of Public Education* (San Francisco: Jossey-Bass, 2008).

37. W. C. Rhoden, *Forty Million Dollar Slaves: The Rise, Fall, and Redemption of the Black Athlete* (New York: Three Rivers Press, 2006).

38. The operation of the conveyor belt in and through college sport is a topic Kristi Oshiro, Anthony Weems, Sayvon Foster, and I tackle in K. Oshiro, et al., "The Operation of the Conveyor Belt in and Through College Sport," in *Racism in College Sport*, 4th ed., ed. D. Brooks and R. Althouse (Morgantown, WV: Fitness Information Technology, forthcoming).

39. D. Sparks and S. K. Robinson, *Lessons of the Game: The Untold Story of High School Football* (Seattle: Game Time Publishing, 1999).

40. The Amateur Athletic Union (AAU) is a youth sports organization that was founded in 1888 to advance the development of youth sports and physical fit-ness programs. AAU basketball started to become popular in the 1980s once major athletic apparel and shoe companies began to sponsor coaches and teams. Teams compete in various national tournaments, typically between March and late July, and elite-level players use these competitions as an oppor-tunity to showcase their talent. Many basketball athletes prioritize AAU over their high school teams because AAU tournaments have become the primary platform for college coaches to recruit. AAU basketball has been criticized for focusing less on the development of players' fundamental skills and more on money and brand image of players and the clubs.

41. W. J. Jordan, "Black High School Students' Participation in School-Sponsored Sports Activities: Effects on School Engagement and Achievement," *Journal of Negro Education* 68, no. 1 (1999): 54–71.

42. J. Zillgitt, "NBA Officially Proposes Lowering Draft Age from 19 to 18," *USA Today*, February 22, 2019.

43. J. R. Gerdy, *Air Ball: American Education's Failed Experiment with Elite Ath-letics* (Jackson, MS: University Press of Mississippi, 2006).

44. J. M. Beyer and D. R. Hannah, "The Cultural Significance of Athletics in US Higher Education," *Journal of Sport Management* 14, no. 2 (2000): 105–132.

45. L. Chalip, "Toward a Distinctive Sport Management Discipline," *Journal of Sport Management* 20, no. 1 (2006): 1–21.

46. *Merriam-Webster's Collegiate Dictionary, Eleventh Edition* (Springfield, MA: Merriam-Webster, Inc., 2008).

47. C. G. Woodson, *The Mis-education of the Negro* (Lexington, KY: Seven Treasures Publications, 1933), 7.
48. M. J. Shujaa, ed., *Too Much Schooling, Too Little Education: A Paradox of Black Life in White Societies* (Trenton, NJ: Africa World Press, 1994).
49. Singer, "The Mis-education of African American Male College Athletes."
50. L. Harrison Jr. et al., "The Mis-education of the African American Student-Athlete," *Kinesiology Review* 6 (2017): 60–69.
51. Ibid.
52. H. R. Milner, *Start Where You Are, but Don't Stay There: Understanding Diversity, Opportunity Gaps, and Teaching in Today's Classrooms* (Cambridge, MA: Harvard Education Press, 2010).

Chapter 2

1. See J. N. Singer, "African American Male College Athletes' Narrative on Education and Racism," *Urban Education* 51, no. 9 (2016): 1065–1095; J. N. Singer, "African American Football Athletes' Perspectives on Institutional Integrity in College Sport," *Research Quarterly for Exercise and Sport* 80, no. 1 (2009): 102–116; J. N. Singer, "Benefits and Detriments of African American Male Athletes' Participation in a Big-Time College Football Program," *International Review for the Sociology of Sport* 43 (2008): 399–408; J. N. Singer, "Understanding Racism Through the Eyes of African American Male Student-Athletes," *Race, Ethnicity and Education* 8 (2005): 365–386.
2. Athletes with true freshman status are those deemed to be freshmen both athletically and academically because they participate in athletic competitions during their first year in college right out of high school. Athletes who redshirt are those who are withheld from participating in athletic competitions during their first or other year in the program so they can further develop their academic and/or athletic skills and extend their eligibility. For example, a running back who redshirts his first year on campus would be considered a sophomore academically during his second year but a redshirt freshman athletically because this would be his first year participating in athletic competitions in the program. Redshirting is fairly common for freshman in Division I programs like the one that is the focus of this chapter or athletes who suffer injuries or other medical hardships during their time in these programs.
3. H. R. Milner, "But What Is Urban Education? *Urban Education* 47, no. 3 (2012): 556–561.
4. C. K. Harrison et al.," Scholar-Baller: Student Athlete Socialization, Motivation, and Academic Performance in American Society," *International Encyclopedia of Education*, vol. 1 (Oxford: Elsevier Ltd., 2010), 860–865.
5. H. Edwards, "The Black 'Dumb Jock': An American Sports Tragedy," *College Board Review* (1984): 8–13.

6. W. E. B. DuBois, *The Souls of Black Folk* (1903; New York: Vintage, 1990).
7. E. Staurowsky and A. Sack, "Reconsidering the Use of the Term Student-Athlete in Academic Research," *Journal of Sport Management* 19, no. 2 (2005): 103–116.
8. A. Zimbalist, *Unpaid Professionals: Commercialism and Conflict in Big-Time College Sport* (Princeton, NJ: Princeton University Press, 1999).
9. K. L. Shropshire and C. D. Williams Jr., *The Miseducation of the Student Athlete: How to Fix College Sports* (Philadelphia: Wharton Digital Press, 2017).
10. See J. H. Greenhaus, S. Parasuraman, and W. M. Wormley, "Effects of Race on Organizational Experiences, Job Performance, Evaluations, and Career Outcomes," *Academy of Management Journal* 33 (1990): 64–86.
11. The big-time college football program where Marcus, Bobby, and Mark played actually had a Black quarterback who split time as a starter with a White quarterback in the mid- to late 1990s.
12. J. N. Cooper, "Excellence Beyond Athletics: Best Practices for Enhancing Black Male Student Athletes' Educational Experiences and Outcomes," *Equity & Excellence in Education* 49, no. 3 (2016): 267–283.
13. K. Beamon, "Racism and Stereotyping on Campus: Experiences of African-American Male Student-Athletes," *Journal of Negro Education* 83, no. 2 (2014): 121–134.
14. O. C. B. Daniels, "Perceiving and Nurturing the Intellectual Development of Black Student-Athletes: A Case of Institutional Integrity," *Western Journal of Black Studies* 11 (1987): 155–163.
15. K. L. Armstrong and M. A. Jennings, "Race, Sport, and Sociocognitive 'Place' in Higher Education: Black Male Student-Athletes as Critical Theorists," *Journal of Black Studies* 49, no. 4 (2018): 358.
16. See E. Comeaux, "Racial Differences in Faculty Perceptions of Collegiate Student-Athletes' Academic and Post-Undergraduate Achievements," *Sociology of Sport Journal* 27, no. 4 (2010): 390–412; E. Comeaux and C. K. Harrison, "A Conceptual Model for Academic Success for Student-Athletes," *Educational Researcher* 40, no. 5 (2011): 235–245; E. Comeaux and C. K. Harrison, "Faculty and Male Student-Athletes: Racial Differences in the Environmental Predictors of Academic Achievement," *Race, Ethnicity, and Education* 10, no. 2 (2007): 199–214.
17. For research on amateurism and athlete compensation, see, for example, A. L. Sack, "Are 'Improper Benefits' Really Improper? A Study of College Athletes' Views Concerning Amateurism," *Journal of Sport and Social Issues* 12 (1988): 1–16; R. G. Schneider and P. M. Pedersen, "Intercollegiate Student-Athletes' Perceptions of Equity: Are Student-Athletes Adequately Rewarded?" *International Journal of Sport Management* 5, no. 1 (2004): 11–26.
18. D. D. Kelly and M. M. Dixon, "Successfully Navigating Life Transitions Among African American Male Student-Athletes: A Review and Examination

of Constellation Mentoring as a Promising Strategy," *Journal of Sport Management* 28 (2014): 498–514.

19. E. Comeaux, ed., *College Athletes' Rights and Well-Being: Critical Perspectives on Policy and Practice* (Baltimore: Johns Hopkins University Press, 2017).

20. J. Bauer-Wolf, "Into the Hands of Athletes—Kind Of," *Inside Higher Ed*, July 6, 2018, http://www.insidehighered.com/news/.

21. G. Ladson-Billings and W. Tate, "Toward a Critical Race Theory of Education," *Teachers College Record* 97 (1995): 47–68.

22. S. Hodge et al., "Theorizing on the Stereotyping of Black Male Student-Athletes," *Journal for the Study of Sports and Athletes in Education* 2, no. 2 (2008): 203–226.

23. K. F. Benson, "Constructing Academic Inadequacy: African American Athletes' Stories of Schooling," *Journal of Higher Education* 71, no. 2 (2000): 223–246.

24. H. Edwards, "The Black 'Dumb Jock': An American Sports Tragedy," *College Board Review* 131 (1984): 8–13.

25. See C. Harris, "Whiteness as Property," *Harvard Law Review* 106, no. 8 (1993): 1709–1791; G. Lipsitz, *The Possessive Investment in Whiteness: How White People Profit from Identity Politics* (Philadelphia: Temple University Press, 2006); P. McIntosh, "White and Male Privilege: A Personal Accounting of Coming to See Correspondences Through Work in Women's Studies," in *Race, Class, and Gender: An Anthology*, ed. M. L. Anderson and P. H. Collins (Belmont, CA: Wadsworth, 1992), 70–81.

26. Research into the stereotyping can be found in B. Hawkins, "Is Stacking Dead? A Case Study of the Stacking Hypothesis at Southeastern Conference (SEC) Football Program," *International Sports Journal*, 6, no. 2 (2002): 146–159; R. Lewis Jr., "Racial Position Segregation: A Case Study of Southwestern Conference Football, 1978 and 1989," *Journal of Black Studies* 25, no. 4 (1995): 431–446.

27. See E. Mercurio and V. F. Filak, "Roughing the Passer: The Framing of Black and White Quarterbacks Prior to the NFL Draft," *Howard Journal of Communications* 21, no. 1 (2010): 56–71; Hodge et al., "Theorizing on the Stereotyping of Black Male Student-Athletes."

28. J. N. Singer, C. K. Harrison, and S. Bukstein, "A Critical Race Analysis of the Hiring Process for Head Coaches in NCAA College Football," *Journal of Intercollegiate Sport* 3 (2010): 270–296; K. J. A. Agyemang and J. DeLorme, "Examining the Dearth of Black Head Football Coaches at the NCAA Football Bowl Subdivision Level: A Critical Race Theory and Social Dominance Theory Analysis," *Journal of Issues in Intercollegiate Athletics* 3 (2010): 35–52.

29. M. K. Asante, *Afrocentricity* (Trenton, NJ: Africa World Press, 1988).

30. A. L. Sack and E. J. Staurowsky, *College Athletes for Hire: The Evolution and Legacy of the NCAA's Amateur Myth* (Westport, CT: Praeger, 1998).

31. Cooper, "Excellence Beyond Athletics."

Chapter 3

1. D. R. Thomas, "A General Inductive Approach for Analyzing Qualitative Evaluation Data," *American Journal of Evaluation* 27, no. 2 (2006): 237–246.

2. J. K. Donnor, "Towards an Interest-Convergence in the Education of African-American Football Student Athletes in Major College Sports," *Race Ethnicity and Education* 8, no. 1 (2005): 45–67.

3. R. A. B. May, *Living Through the Hoop: High School Basketball, Race, and the American Dream* (New York: New York University Press, 2008).

4. E. Comeaux, "The Student(less) Athlete: Identifying the Unidentified College Student," *Journal for the Study of Sports and Athletes in Education* 1, no. 1 (2007): 37–44.

5. G. Ladson-Billings, "Toward a Theory of Culturally Relevant Pedagogy," *American Education Research Journal* 35 (1995): 465–491.

6. H. R. Milner, *Start Where You Are, but Don't Stay There: Understanding Diversity, Opportunity Gaps, and Teaching in Today's Classrooms* (Cambridge, MA: Harvard Education Press, 2010).

7. M. J. Shujaa, ed., *Too Much Schooling, Too Little Education: A Paradox of Black Life in White Societies* (Trenton, NJ: Africa World Press, 1994).

8. B. D. Tatum, *Why Are All The Black Kids Sitting Together in the Cafeteria? And Other Conversations About Race* (New York: Basic Books, 1997).

9. J. N. Singer and G. B. Cunningham, "A Case Study of the Diversity Culture of an American University Athletic Department: Perceptions of Senior Level Administrators," *Sport, Education, and Society* 17, no. 5 (2012): 647–669.

10. J. Gaston Gayles et al., "Neoliberal Capitalism and Racism in College Athletics: Critical Approaches for Supporting Student-Athletes," *New Directions for Student Services* 2018, no. 163 (2018): 11–21.

11. J. N. Singer and G. B. Cunningham, "A Collective Case Study of African American Male Athletic Directors' Leadership Approaches to Diversity in College Sport," *Journal of Intercollegiate Sport* 11, no. 2 (2018): 269–297.

12. L. Harrison Jr. et al, "Living the Dream or Awakening from the Nightmare: Race and Athletic Identity," *Race, Ethnicity and Education* 14, no. 1 (2011): 91–103; A. Y. Bimper and L. Harrison, "Meet Me at the Crossroads: African American Athletic and Racial Identity," *Quest* 63, no. 3 (2011): 275–288.

13. A. J. M. Pabon, "Waiting for Black Superman: A Look at a Problematic Assumption," *Urban Education* 51, no. 8 (2016): 915–939; A. J. M. Pabon, N. S. Anderson, and H. Kharem, "Minding the Gap: Cultivating Black Male Teachers in a Time of Crisis in Urban Schools," *Journal of Negro Education* 80, no. 3 (2011): 358–367.

14. J. N. Cooper et al., "Collective Uplift: The Impact of a Holistic Development Support Program on Black Male Former College Athletes' Experiences and Outcomes," *International Journal of Qualitative Studies in Education* (2018), doi:10.1080/09518398.2018.1522011.

15. J. N. Cooper and B. Hawkins, "An Anti-Deficit Perspective on Black Male Student Athletes' Educational Experiences at a Historically Black College/University," *Race, Ethnicity and Education* (2014), doi:10.1080/13613324.2014.946491.
16. D. Pragman, "End the Charade: Let Athletes Major in Sports," *Chronicle of Higher Education*, November 26, 2012, https://www.chronicle.com/article/End-the-Charade-Let-Athletes/135894.
17. Hawkins, *The New Plantation: Black Athletes, College Sports, and Predominantly White NCAA Institutions* (New York: Palgrave MacMillan, 2010).
18. For an interesting perspective on this matter, see J. M. Smith and M. Willingham, *Cheated: The UNC Scandal, the Education of Athletes, and the Future of Big-Time College Sports* (Lincoln, NE: Potomac Books, 2015).

Chapter 4

1. H. Edwards, "Crisis of Black Athletes on the Eve of the 21st Century," *Society* (March/April 2000): 9–12.
2. M. Chesler, A. E. Lewis, and J. E. Crowfoot, *Challenging Racism in Higher Education: Promoting Justice* (Lanham, MD: Rowman & Littlefield, 2005), 47.
3. The Notorious B.I.G, "Juicy" [Recorded by The Notorious B.I.G.], on *Ready to Die* (New York: Bad Boy and Arista,), CD.
4. J. N. Cooper, *From Exploitation Back to Empowerment: Black Male Holistic (Under) Development Through Sport and (Mis)Education* (New York: Peter Lang, 2019).
5. J. Feagin and K. Ducey, *Elite White Men Ruling: Who, What, When, Where, and How* (New York: Routledge, 2017).
6. See S. Eitzen, "Racism in Big-Time College Sport: Prospects for the Year 2020 and Proposals for Change," in *Racism in College Athletics: The African American Athlete's Experience* (2nd ed.), ed. D. Brooks and R. Althouse (Morgantown, WV: Fitness Information Technology, 2000), 293–306.
7. I once had a lengthy conversation with an athletic director at a major Division I HWCU who referred to these athletes at his institution as valuable "products" that he needed to make sure were taken care of and available to produce on the fields and courts.
8. See J. R. Feagin, *Systemic Racism: A Theory of Oppression* (New York: Routledge, 2006)
9. D. Bell, *Faces at the Bottom of the Well: The Permanence of Racism* (New York: Basic Books, 1992).
10. W. H. Watkins, *The White Architects of Black Education: Ideology and Power in America, 1865–1954* (New York: Teachers College Press, 2001), 1–2.
11. M. J. Shujaa, ed., *Too Much Schooling, Too Little Education: A Paradox of Black Life in White Societies* (Trenton, NJ: Africa World Press, 1994).

12. In a short case study at the beginning of a chapter on the miseducation of African American male college athletes, I briefly discuss how young Black male athletes' issues and challenges with literacy are arguably rooted in the historical laws that prohibited Blacks from learning how to read and write during slavery; see J. N. Singer, "The Mis-education of African American Male College Athletes," in *Introduction to Intercollegiate Athletics*, ed. E. Comeaux (Baltimore: Johns Hopkins University Press, 2015), 193–206.

13. See T. Davis, "The Myth of the Superspade: The Persistence of Racism in College Athletics," *Fordham Urban Law Journal* 22 (1995): 615–698.

14. J. Donnor, "Towards an Interest-Convergence in The Education of African-American Football Student Athletes in Major College Sports," in *Race, Ethnicity and Education* 8, no. 1 (2005): 45–67.

15. B. Osborne, "The Myth of the Exploited Student-Athlete," *Journal of Intercollegiate Sport* 7 (2014): 143–152.

16. D. Van Rheenen, "Exploitation in College Sports: Race, Revenue, and Educational Reward," *International Review for the Sociology of Sport* 48, no. 5 (2012): 550–571.

17. B. Hawkins, *The New Plantation: Black Athletes, College Sports, and Predominantly White NCAA Institutions* (New York: Palgrave MacMillan, 2010).

18. See T. Slack and M. M. Parent *Understanding Sport Organizations: The Application of Organization Theory*, 2nd ed. (Champaign, IL: Human Kinetics, 2006); and W. Frisby, "The Good, the Bad, and the Ugly: Critical Sport Management Research," in *Journal of Sport Management* 19, no. 1 (2005): 1–12.

19. G. Morgan, *Images of Organizations* (Beverly Hills, CA: Sage, 1986).

20. U. M. Jayakumar and E. Comeaux, "The Cultural Cover-Up of College Athletics: How Organizational Culture Perpetuates an Unrealistic and Idealized Balancing Act," *Journal of Higher Education* 87, no. 4 (2016): 488–515.

21. C. Spigner, "African American Student-Athletes: Academic Support or Institutionalized Racism?" *Education* 114, no. 1 (1993): 144–150.

22. See, for example, L. A. Kihl, T. Richardson, and C. Campisi, "Toward a Grounded Theory of Student-Athlete Suffering and Dealing with Academic Corruption," *Journal of Sport Management* 22 (2008): 273–302.

23. S. Allen, "Buzz Williams Taught His Players to Respect the National Anthem," *Washington Post*, March 10, 2016.

24. Eurocentric organizations are typically White male controlled and promote European values and interests. These types of organizations are based on a Western orientation toward materialism, hierarchal control, bottom-line profits, hyper-competition and aggression, individualism, narcissism, and the overconsumption of natural resources and material goods. See K. Nunn, "Law as a Eurocentric Enterprise," *Law & Inequality* 15 (1997): 323; and N. Warfield-Coppock, "Toward a Theory of Afrocenric Organizations," *Journal of Black Psychology* 21, no. 30 (1995): 30–48.

25. J. R. Feagin, *The White Racial Frame: Centuries of Racial Framing and Counter-Framing*, 2nd ed. (New York: Routledge, 2013).
26. R. Southall and E. Staurowsky, "Cheering on the Collegiate Model: Creating, Disseminating, and Imbedding the NCAA's Redefinition of Amateurism," *Journal of Sport and Social Issues* 37, no. 4 (2013): 403–429.
27. D. Meggyesy, "Athletes in Big-Time College Sport," *Society* (2000): 24–28.
28. Southall and Staurowsky, "Cheering on the Collegiate Model."
29. See G. Sailes, "An Investigation of Campus Stereotypes: The Myth of Black Athletic Superiority and the Dumb Jock Stereotype," *Sociology of Sport Journal* 10 (1993): 88–97; R. Hughes, J. Satterfield, and M. Giles, "Athleticizing Black Male Student-Athletes: The Social Construction of Race, Sports, Myths, and Realities," *NASAP Journal* 10, no. 1 (2007): 112–127.
30. S. Hodge, et al., "Theorizing on the Stereotyping of Black Male Student-Athletes," *Journal for the Study of Sports and Athletes in Education* 2, no. 2 (2008): 203–226. These scholars utilized social psychologist James Jones's psychological version of CRT to account for the role of social psychological processes in the continuing racial disparities between black athletes and their white counterparts.
31. Ibid., 218.
32. See K. L. Armstrong and M. A. Jennings, "Race, Sport, and Sociocognitive 'Place' in Higher Education: Black Male Student-Athletes as Critical Theorists," *Journal of Black Studies* 49, no. 4 (2018): 349–369.
33. A. Y. Bimper Jr. and L. Harrison Jr., " Are We Committed to Issues of Race? Institutional Integrity Across Intercollegiate Athletics," *International Review for the Sociology of Sport* (2015): 1–18.
34. See J. N Cooper, "Strategic Navigation: A Comparative Study of Black Male Scholar Athletes' Experiences at a Historically Black College/University (HBCU) and Historically White University (HWU)," *International Journal of Qualitative Studies in Education* 31, no. 4 (2017): 235–256; J. N. Cooper, C. J. Porter, and T. J. Davis, "Success Through Community Cultural Wealth: Reflections from Black Female College Athletes at a Historically Black College/University (HBCU) and Historically White Institution (HWI)," *Journal of Intercollegiate Sport* 10, no. 2 (2017): 129–156; J. N. Cooper, "A Culture of Collective Uplift: The Influence of a Historically Black College/University on Black Male Student Athletes' Experiences," *Journal of Issues in Intercollegiate Athletics* 6 (2013): 306–331.
35. For one such source of data, see American Institutes for Research, *Report No. 3: The Experiences of Black Intercollegiate Athletes at NCAA Division I Institutions* (Palo Alto, CA: Center for the Study of Athletics, 1989).
36. Prior to 1972, first-year freshman football and basketball athletes were not eligible to compete in athletic competition. The idea was that freshman ineligibility would allow these athletes a year to better adjust to the academic and

other demands of higher education without having to juggle athletic and academic responsibilities. Interestingly, the elimination of the freshman ineligibility policy corresponded with the beginnings of the mass influx of Black male athletes into football and basketball programs at HWCU.

37. See K. L. Shropshire and Colin D. Williams, *The Miseducation of the Student-Athlete: How to Fix College Sports* (Philadelphia: Wharton Digital Press, 2017).

38. B. Hawkins, *The New Plantation: Black Athletes, College Sports, and Predominantly White NCAA Institutions* (New York: Palgrave MacMillan, 2010), 176.

39. Shropshire and Williams, *The Miseducation of the Student-Athlete*.

40. T. Yosso, "Whose Culture Has Capital? A Critical Race Theory Discussion of Community Cultural Wealth," *Race Ethnicity and Education* 8, no. 1 (2005): 69–91. According to Yosso, *aspirational capital* refers to the ability to be resilient and to hold onto hopes and dreams in the face adversity; *linguistic capital* refers to language and communication skills and styles; *familial capital* refers to cultural knowledge that is nurtured through immediate family and home communities; *social capital* refers to networks of people and community resources; *navigational capital* refers to the ability to maneuver through social institutions; *resistant capital* refers to knowledge and skills developed through the engagement in oppositional behavior that challenges inequity and inequality.

41. See K. Novak, *UDL Now! A Teacher's Guide to Applying Universal Design for Learning in Today's Classrooms* (Wakefield, MA: CAST Professional Publishing, 2016).

42. C. West, *Race Matters* (New York: Vintage Books, 1993), 6.

43. J. N. Cooper et al., "Collective Uplift: The Impact of a Holistic Development Support Program on Black Male Former College Athletes' Experiences and Outcomes," *International Journal of Qualitative Studies in Education* 32, no. 1 (2019): 21–46.

44. J. N. Cooper, A. Nwadike, and C. Macaulay, "A Critical Race Theory Analysis of Big-Time College Sports: Implications for Culturally Responsive and Race-Conscious Sport Leadership," *Journal of Issues in Intercollegiate Athletics* 10 (2017): 204–233.

45. T. Carter, dir., *Coach Carter* [Motion picture] (Hollywood, CA: Paramount Pictures, 2005).

46. See B. B. Douglas, E. Pitre, and C. W. Lewis, "African American Male Student-Athletes and White Teachers' Classroom Interactions: Implications for Teachers, Coaches, Counselors, and Administrators," in *White Teachers/Diverse Classrooms: A Guide to Building Inclusive Schools, Promoting High Expectations, and Eliminating Racism*, ed. J. Landsman and C. W. Lewis (Sterling, VA: Stylus, 2006), 137–149.

Acknowledgments

ALTHOUGH THERE IS NOT ENOUGH SPACE HERE to explicitly mention everyone who has contributed in some way, shape, or form to my growth and development from birth to when I finished writing this book, I do recognize that countless people have inspired or assisted me, directly or indirectly, in this personal and professional life journey. I want to acknowledge and thank the many graduate and undergraduate students I have taught/mentored and learned from during my time as a faculty member in higher education; and all those teachers, administrators, coaches, peers, colleagues, friends and acquaintances, and even strangers who have, knowingly or unknowingly, played some significant role in this journey. I am particularly thankful that my doctoral advisor from The Ohio State University, Ketra Armstrong, accepted me into the sport management doctoral program, and provided me a space to do this important work related to Black male college athletes.

That being said, I do want to specifically acknowledge some of the people who really helped make this book project become a reality. First and foremost, I want to thank Doug Clayton and the staff at Harvard Education Press for believing in the idea for this book and offering me the opportunity to publish my work with such a highly respected publisher. Doug, I especially appreciate your understanding, patience, and willingness to work with me as I struggled to bring closure to this project. Your feedback and encouragement throughout this process was certainly helpful. Many thanks to the editorial and production director, Chris Leonesio; the marketing manager, Laura Cutone Godwin; and copyeditor, Monica Jainschigg, for working with me to streamline and better focus this project. I was quite pleased with the finished product!

I also thank the two external reviewers who provided invaluable feedback on the original proposal I submitted to Harvard Education Press. Your advice that I centralize the voices of Black male athletes in the book helped me (re)focus my efforts and this made the book all the better. In that vein, I must certainly thank the Black males whose stories and perspectives are featured in this book. Your willingness to participate in my research for this book project and allow me to (re)present your powerful and important voices in these pages is what elevated this project to where it needed to be!

I would be remiss in my duty if I did not thank my brother from another mother, kindred spirit, and best of friends Rich Milner for pushing me over many years to believe in myself and see my potential to author a solo book project like this. Thank you for introducing me to Doug and his colleagues at Harvard Education Press and encouraging them to consider this project. Since we first met in 2000 at The Ohio State University as doctoral students in that statistics course, you have supported me, motivated me, and continue to inspire me to be the very best I can in both my personal and professional life. I appreciate all you have done for me and meant to me over the years and will always be eternally grateful for our friendship and brotherhood.

I also want to send a special shout-out and acknowledgment to my friend and colleague Daniella Cook, whom I first met at the Critical Race Studies in Education conference in San Antonio, Texas, in 2011. After listening to my presentation on Black male college athletes, you approached and really helped me to see that I had a book project on my hands. Our many conversations going forward were instrumental in helping me further develop ideas for this book. It is my hope that I can one day be as skillful and nuanced as you are when it comes to creating and utilizing composite characters to creatively challenge dominant methodological and epistemological canons in education research. Thank you for your brilliance, and the support you have given me over the years, my friend!

I must also acknowledge Betty Sanford, who was the coordinator of the Summer University Program Excellence Required (SUPER) bridge program for several years at my alma mater, Michigan State University. Betty hired me as a graduate assistant when I returned to MSU to pursue a master's degree, and it was during that time that I began working as an adviser and mentor to several Black male college athletes who participated in this program. As I discuss in this book, I attribute much of my initial interest in the study of and with Black male college athletes to this transformative experience. Betty, I really appreciated the opportunity to work with and learn from you over those three summers I worked in the program, and I've grown to see you as an extension of family. It was such an honor and delight to have you and your husband, John, make the trip to Texas to celebrate with me on my wedding day.

I also want to acknowledge all the football and basketball athletes who came through SUPER during my time as a graduate assistant for this program, particularly Alex Auston. Alex, our initial encounters during your early days in the program were under less-than-ideal or -desirable circumstances, but once we established trust between us, our relationship blossomed and we had some very positive and powerful interactions and experiences. Of particular note was the road trip you, Jeff, Baron Jay, Oneil, and I took to Chicago to hear The Minister speak.

Last, but certainly not least, I acknowledge my family, particularly my late paternal grandparents, John William Singer and Helen Mae Singer; late maternal grandparents, Wendell Macon and Mollie Mae Macon; my father, Johnny J. Singer, and mother, Apostle Vera J. Cole. You all serve as the foundation of it all, and I am because you were and are. I also acknowledge my sisters, Jamie and Natalie, and baby brother and best friend, Marcus, as well as the many uncles (particularly Vinton, Terry, and David), aunts (particularly Sherri, my fellow Michigan State University alum), cousins (particularly Aaron Michael), nieces, and nephews.

But most importantly, I want to thank my wonderful wife and life partner, Shauntā Lindsey Singer. It is such a blessing and awesome responsibility for me to share this life with you and our two beautiful baby daughters, Journey Justice and Jordyn Truth. Thank you for loving and supporting me in my attempts to juggle and balance the demands of being a great husband and father, an authentic scholar, educator, and leader in the academy, and the best intercollegiate and interscholastic basketball official possible. Thank you for suffeRING through my grumpy moods during the challenging process of writing this book! Thank you for enduRING the many long days and nights you had to pick up the slack when I was not physically or mentally present or engaged in family affairs! Thank you for sometimes cateRING to me when I needed that extra push to make it through this long, but ultimately rewarding process! I am thankful to Almighty God for sending you into my life path, and giving me you as the HELP MEET I need to clarify and fulfill my mission and purpose in life.

About the Author

John N. Singer is associate professor of sport management in the Department of Health and Kinesiology and associate dean for diversity and inclusion within the College of Education and Human Development at Texas A&M University. He is also an affiliate faculty of the Institute for the Study of Sport, Society, and Social Change at San Jose State University. Dr. Singer's research and scholarly interests have primarily centered around the intersections between race, sport, and education, with a keen focus on the complex and contextual realities Black males face as primary stakeholders in organized school sport. His work has also been concerned with diversity and social justice matters in sporting institutions and organizations, with an emphasis on the experiences, mind-sets, and plight of historically underrepresented and marginalized groups. Dr. Singer's work has appeared in numerous peer-reviewed academic journals, including the *Journal of Sport Management*; *Journal of Intercollegiate Sport*; *International Review for the Sociology of Sport*; *Sport, Education, & Society*; *Journal of Black Studies*; *Urban Education*; and *Race, Ethnicity, and Education*. He has also contributed to the literature as the author of numerous chapters in edited books across the fields of education, sociology, sport studies, and sport management. Dr. Singer received the Montague Scholar-Center for Teaching Excellence Award at Texas A&M in 2009, and the North American Society of Sport Management Diversity Award in 2019. He received his PhD from The Ohio State University.

Index